Labor Legislation from an Economic Point of View

LIBERTY FUND, INC.
Indianapolis, Indiana

Labor Legislation from an Economic Point of View

GUSTAVO R. VELASCO

Edited and with an introduction by
B. A. ROGGE
Distinguished professor of Political Economy
Wabash College

LIBERTY FUND, INC.
Indianapolis, Indiana

Printed in the United States of America

Contents

Introduction

by

B. A. ROGGE

PROFESSOR VELASCO IS NO STRANGER TO CONTROVERSY, NOR TO finding himself standing virtually alone in defense of his position. He has long stood for free markets and free men in a nation where the ruling party has been formally socialist and in a world where the ruling practice has been somewhere between the interventionist and the socialist.

In this monograph, he takes on one of the most durable and widely held interpretations of capitalist experience, an interpretation that goes as follows: Whatever may be the *ultimate* impact on human welfare of the coming of capitalism in a given country, the immediate and intermediate consequences tend to be disadvantageous to the great masses of the people and particularly to the workers, i.e. to those who represent the man and woman-power of the newly developing factory system. In some cases, their *absolute* levels of living may be reduced, relative to the pre-capitalist period; in all cases, they suffer a decline in *relative* well-being, as the lion's share of the gains from industrialization go to the owners of the means of production. In addition as they leave the home workshop or the peasant farm for the factory, they are no longer using tools of their own possession for the production of goods for their own use or for direct exchange within the community; they use tools owned by others for the production of "commodities," that is of things to be exchanged for money in the open market place. In so doing they become alienated from their work; this sense of alienation comes to pervade their whole beings and they lose the dignity that is the proper lot of man.

Low wages, long hours, unsafe and unhealthy working conditions, child labor and female labor and sweated labor, alienation and despair—such is the lot of the working class under capitalism, *unless* . . . Unless what? Unless the state intervenes with direct legislation controlling hours and conditions of work, wages to be paid, etc. and unless the state gives positive and special assistance to the self-help activities of the workers in the form of labor unions.

The two central questions posed in this interpretation of capitalist experience are the following: What *in fact* has been the lot of the worker under early, middle and late capitalism? and What *in fact* has been the impact of labor legislation (and the trade union) on the position of the worker under capitalism?

Those who wish to explore an answer to the first of these two questions that runs counter to the position described above can do no better than examine *Capitalism and the Historians*, edited by F. A. Hayek[1]. Those who wish to explore an answer to the second of these two questions that runs counter to the one described above can do no better than examine the pages to follow. Velasco presents his own position early and unequivocally. On the second page of his manuscript, he writes as follows:

> The sorry truth is that this modern dogma, this fond illusion that through official orders and union pressure we can raise the standard of living of the largest part of the population and that most deserving of help, is false. And not only is it false; it is harmful as well, because prolabor policies produce results that are exactly the opposite of those their proponents pursue. In other words, instead of making a nation richer, they make it poorer; instead of be-

[1] F. A. Hayek, *Capitalism and the Historians*, University of Chicago, 1954.

Introduction

ing a factor for progress, they are a brake on it; instead of
increasing welfare, they hinder and deter it.

I direct your attention to the fact that this position of Velasco's
is not a "point of view," i.e. a value judgment, but a scientific
judgment, a particular interpretation of the evidence. It may
be wrong but, if so, it is wrong not as a matter of taste or pre-
ference but as a matter of fact. I must note that the Velasco
reading of the evidence is confirmed not only by my own reading of that evidence but by the findings of many who have
turned their professional attention to this question in recent
decades. Thus, Professor Albert Rees has concluded,

> Perhaps the best summary statement that can be made
> from the available evidence about the effect of unions on
> the size distribution of income is that unions have probably
> raised many higher income workers from an initial position
> somewhat above the middle of the income distribution to
> a present position closer to the top. They have narrowed
> the gap between the best paid manual workers and the
> very rich, and widened the gap between these workers and
> the very poor. This effect cannot be completely described
> by calling it either an increase or a decrease in the equality
> of income distribution, though it seems closer to the latter
> than to the former.[2]

In the same vein, Professor Milton Friedman writes:

> If unions raise wage rates in a particular occupation or
> industry, they necessarily make the amount of employment
> available in that occupation or industry less than it other-
> wise would be—just as any higher price cuts down the
> amount purchased. The effect is an increased number of
> persons seeking other jobs, which forces down wages in
> other occupations. Since unions have generally been
> strongest among groups that would have been high-paid
> anyway, their effect has been to make high-paid workers

[2]Albert Rees, *The Economics of Trade Unions*, The University of Chicago
Press, Phoenix Books, Chicago, 1967, pp. 98–9.

higher paid at the expense of the lower-paid workers. Unions have therefore not only harmed the public at large and workers as a whole by distorting the use of labor; they have also made the incomes of the working class more unequal by reducing the opportunities available to the most disadvantaged workers.[3]

Not the least of those who have been damaged by trade union actions have been the minority race groups in this (and other) countries. Thus, the Labor Secretary of the NAACP has written,

> "In the last years of the nineteenth century and in the first decades of the twentieth, the harsh discriminatory racial practices of AFL-affiliated unions and the railroad brotherhoods were decisive factors in developing the pattern of Negro job limitation that was to continue for many generations."[4]

More recently the distinguished Jamaica-born black economist, Sir Arthur Lewis, now teaching at Princeton University has said, "The trade unions are the black man's greatest enemy in the United States."[5]

Admittedly all so-called proofs of hypotheses are only statements of probabilities, more or less certain, and the Velasco thesis could be wrong. But I am convinced that not only is it almost certainly correct but that through this hypothesis, he has helped to explain much of the chaos that now infects modern and not-so-modern and would-be modern societies. With Velasco, I am convinced that no single error has done so much to produce mistaken, even tragically mistaken legislative action as this twin myth of labor exploitation and of the trade union as the saving agency. Almost every problem of the countries of this day reflects its impact, whether the problem be

[3]Milton Friedman, *Capitalism and Freedom*, University of Chicago Press, Phoenix Books, Chicago, 1962, p. 124.

[4]Herbert Hill, "The Racial Practices of Organized Labor—the Age of Gompers and After," in Ross and Hill, *Employment, Race and Poverty*, New York: Harcourt, Brace and World, 1967, pp. 365–6.

[5]Sir Arthur Lewis, Chicago *Tribune*, May 11, 1969, p. 2, sect. 1.

that of inflation or balance of payments disequilibria or unemployment or residual poverty or racial income imbalance. The very survival of a reasonably free and reasonably prosperous sector in an unfree and unprosperous world may well depend on a greater acceptance and more meaningful response to the message that Professor Velasco brings us in the pages to follow.

Labor Legislation from an Economic Point of View

———

LIBERTY FUND, INC.
Indianapolis, Indiana

*No society can surely be flourishing
and happy, of which the far greater
part of its members are poor and miserable.*

ADAM SMITH, *The Wealth of Nations*,
BOOK I, CHAPTER VIII.

Chapter I

"LABOR LEGISLATION WITH A MARKEDLY PROTECTIONIST CHAR-
acter constitutes one of the essential features of our times."[1]
This sentence is found in the statement of purposes of the bill
that the President of the Republic sent to the Mexican Con-
gress in March of 1931 and that some months later was enacted
as the Federal Labor Law which is still in force. Whether we
like it or not, it expresses an undeniable truth. Although someone has suggested that we call our age "the era of socialism," it
would be more nearly correct, in my opinion, to name it "the era
of labor or of laborism." The reason for this is that socialism still
raises certain doubts or provokes some opposition, whereas the
prolabor policy that governments have followed almost without exception for over a century has won nearly unanimous
acceptance, especially since around 1917, when the Mexican
Revolution had the distinction "of showing the world that it
was the first to include in a constitution the sacred rights of
the workers," as representative Alfonso Cravioto proclaimed.[2]
Efforts are made to curb its excesses; the inequities and immo-

[1]Department of Industry, Commerce, and Labor, *Draft for the Federal Labor
Law*, Government Printing Office, Mexico, 1931, p. X.
[2]*Journal of the Discussions in the Constitutional Convention*, Printing Office of
the House of Representatives, Mexico, 1922, v.I, p. 720.

1

ralities which it has favored are criticized, especially when they are committed by some union leaders, while other persons regret its use for political purposes; but the principle itself, that is, the belief that government action is capable of improving the condition of the workers, is never disputed. Even employers do not offer the least ideological resistance to it, in spite of the fact that they are its front-line victims (in the final analysis we all are, and especially, the workers, who are the ones that suffer the most). Instead, they limit themselves to a defensive action, to rear-guard skirmishes in which they discuss quantitative matters, that is, how much they can raise wages, but never fundamental or theoretical problems.

The sorry truth is that this modern dogma, this fond illusion that through official orders and union pressure we can raise the standard of living of the largest part of the population and that most deserving of help, is false. And not only is it false; it is harmful as well, because prolabor policies produce results that are exactly the opposite of those their proponents pursue. In other words, instead of making a nation richer, they make it poorer; instead of being a factor for progress, they are a brake on it; instead of increasing welfare, they hinder and deter it.

It is not love of sensationalism that leads me to make the foregoing statements in such brief and energetic terms. What I would like is to shake off the mental torpor that has come over us in this matter and to force all of us to think about it again. Far from seeking any personal advantage through the attitude which I adopt, I fully realize that it will result only in personal attacks and other unpleasantness. "Questioning the virtues of the organized labor movement," writes an economist, "is like attacking religion, monogamy, motherhood, or the home. Among the modern intelligentsia any doubts about collective bargaining admit of explanation only in terms of insanity, knavery, or subservience to the 'interests.' Discussion of skeptical views runs almost entirely in terms of how one came by such persuasions, as though they were symptoms of disease."[3]

[3]Simons, Henry C., "Some Reflections on Syndicalism," in *Economic Policy for a Free Society*. The University of Chicago Press, Chicago, 1948, p. 121.

For these reasons I consider it worthwhile to clear up some points from the outset. In the first place, I wish to emphasize that my opinions are purely personal, for which reason neither the schools nor any of the organizations with which I am connected nor the persons who are my friends can be held responsible for them. Secondly, I must stress that no one is more interested than I am in improving the situation of the working classes, of which I consider myself a member, since I began to work while in school and hope to die working. It is precisely because my purpose is that the income of workers should increase as much as possible and that their situation should become more favorable in every possible respect that I have decided to study labor problems from a point of view which is not that of my specialty as a lawyer and law teacher.

My last explanation may serve to determine the purpose and contents of this study. I sincerely believe that I may count myself among the true friends of the laboring classes (I make this reservation because some people use them to become rich, to gain power, or to transform the liberal, democratic, capitalistic system of organization under which we still live), and that no difference separates us with regard to the ends to be sought. Our lack of agreement refers to the means and more specifically to the thesis that "the improvement in the material conditions of labor, the rise in real wages, the shortening of the hours of work, the abolition of child labor and all other 'social gains' are achievements of government prolabor legislation. But for the interference of the government and the unions the conditions of the laboring class would be as bad as they were in the early period of the Industrial Revolution."[4] This is the only economic problem which arises and which it is worthwhile to investigate. Once again, it is not in question whether more well-being for the masses is desirable. My unequivocal opinion is that it is. On the other hand, I believe that the means that traditional prolabor policy has employed for this end are not only not the appropriate ones, but precisely self-defeating. This is what I shall try to demonstrate.

[4]Mises, Ludwig von, *The Objectives of Economic Education*, Technological Institute of Mexico, p. 20.

The "Labor Is Not A Commodity" Argument

"Thinking has become so emotional and so politically biased on the subject of wages that in most discussions of them the plainest principles are ignored," remarks an economist. "People who would be among the first to deny that prosperity could be brought about by artificially boosting prices . . . will nevertheless advocate minimum wage laws and denounce opponents of them, without misgivings."[5] It even appears as if a psycho-pathological process took place in regard to this subject, as a result of which what is certain and apparent in economics in general ceases to be so as soon as one enters the field of labor relations. This makes it necessary to set ourselves some prior questions, with a view to confirming that we are faced by economic problems and that these problems are capable of being elucidated with the help of the theory elaborated for the purpose.

In contradiction to this possibility, or at least in contrast to the logical rigor that is required by scientific work, it is asserted that labor is not a commodity and that wages are not prices. These statements are chiefly found in such vulgarizations of economics as inspire most of my colleagues who deal with labor law, but instances can be cited of respectable documents, such as the section of the Treaty of Versailles that established the International Labor Organization. Such documents have contributed to their diffusion.[6] Notwithstanding the consideration we owe to their authors, as well as to the lofty purposes that presumably impelled them, we must answer definitely and firmly that they are mistaken. That every man is his own master and that even if he wished it, he cannot be sold or bought, are, of course, accepted maxims of Western civilization (although I must remark incidentally that they were put into effect only in quite recent times). But it does not follow

[5]Hazlitt, Henry, *Economics in One Lesson,* Harper and Brothers. New York and London, 1946, p. 137.

[6]Section II, General Principles, Article 427 (quoted in *Reorganization of Social Economy,* by Oswald Von Nell Bruening, S.J., The Bruce Publishing Company, New York, Milwaukee, Chicago, 1939, p. 38).

4

from this principle of inalienability, or from the fact that a laborer cannot become a chattel, that his services cannot be bought and sold. Let us begin by specifying, since this will aid us to think more clearly, that it is not his work in general or in the abstract that a man engages himself to provide, but only certain services and more concretely certain realizations, certain results of work. In the next place, it is undeniable that work, in the limited sense which I have here defined, constitutes a factor of production; that it is scarce; and that men behave with regard to it in the same way that they do with respect to other scarce productive factors. Consequently, the conclusion that work is bought and sold in the market and that it is a commodity in this meaning of the word, represents nothing more than the enunciation or acknowledgment of a fact.

Similarly, if we define prices as the rates at which money is exchanged for goods or services, one will be forced to admit as well that a wage is in effect a price. The only thing to be regretted is that our language should have coined a special term in order to designate the price of work, because this circumstance is responsible for a good part of the difficulty which surrounds rigorous thought about these matters. Let us remember, however, that what we finally expect, even from things, from material goods, are certain services, certain attributes. These services are obtained sometimes through purchase, at other times by means of a lease, at still other times as a result of contracts or arrangements which bear other names. When what is obtained is the services of a horse, one pays a price or a rent (according to whether they are acquired permanently or temporarily); in the case of a lawyer, one pays a fee; in that of office workers, salaries; in that of manual laborers, wages. But the variety of names should not lead us to believe that the concepts to which they apply are different, if economic analysis does not find any disparities between them.

In view of the foregoing, the reluctance to use accepted terminology can be due only to sentimental reasons. Let us admit that work should not be designated as a commodity, nor wages as prices. Will they in this way escape from economic regularities? Assuredly man is not an animal; much less is he a physical object. But who will deny the existence of biological laws, to whose operation we are subject? Who will dare to jump through a window, with the assurance that his human quality will free him from the tyranny of physical laws, which cause other bodies to be shattered to pieces against the pavement?

The "Exploitation" Argument

A more cautious opinion admits that neither work nor its compensation can escape from the application of economic laws, but holds that man can, and should, prevent or correct the consequences that derive from their being allowed to operate freely. Its central argument is to the effect that workers are exploited, in the sense that normally they receive in exchange for their efforts an amount that is lower than what should belong to them. In turn, this theory is based on the "weakness" of the worker, in face of the "strength" of the employer, which results in disadvantageous bargaining and forces the first party to accept the salary fixed by the second one, to the benefit of the latter and to the detriment of the former.

I shall deal later on with the possibility of setting wages higher than those determined by a market, or rather with its economic effects, because the possibility of so doing, in the absolute sense of the word, cannot be called into question. For the moment I shall discuss this very important thesis of the exploitation of labor and of its alleged inferiority when bargaining with those who have need of its services. I shall do this at length, since this thesis is widely diffused and is repeated as if it were self-evident, and since even reputed economists, whom one should suppose capable of perceiving that it is not correct, subscribe to it. Finally, I consider that this belief (that workers get the worst part when an economy is allowed to operate freely) is what furnishes the chief explanation of the inconsistencies and contradictions to which I referred above, on the part of persons who in other instances possess the perceptiveness and intellectual vigor that are necessary to follow and to understand the reasonings of economic theory.

Let us start with the disadvantage of the worker, which in general is supposed to be the fault of freedom or of competition. For example, its most eloquent expounder, Father Lacordaire, tells us in his well-known phrase that "between the weak and the strong, between the rich and the poor, it is freedom that destroys, it is the law which redeems."[7] And the Webbs, those holy persons of British trade-unionism, hold that the fundamental objective of labor unions should be "the deliberate regulation of conditions of employment in such a way as to ward off from the manual working producers the evil effects of industrial competition."[8]

It is unfortunate that in these statements, as well as in others that I could quote, form is superior to content, and the striving after rhetorical effect much greater than their scientific value. We need not dwell either on the impropriety of restoring, for purposes of economic demonstration, to such vague terms as "weak" and "strong." It is obvious that nothing is gained through denouncing freedom and competition. One should go farther and investigate what concrete circumstances determine that freedom and competition should yield bad results in labor matters.

According to opinions that I shall try to present with the same faithfulness with which I have quoted other more forceful expressions in favor of the viewpoints that I am examining, a workman is forced to sell his capacity to work at any price that he can get because:

(a) He has no other sources of income and is unable to wait, while the employer can fall back on reserves.

[7] Quoted by several authors, for instance, by Henri Decugis, *Les Etapes du Droit*, Sirey, Paris, 1946, v.I.

[8] Webb, Sidney and Beatrice, *Industrial Democracy*, Longmans, Green and Co., Ltd., New York, 1926, p. 807.

(b) Work is a perishable good, which must be sold today or will have disappeared by tomorrow.

(c) Employers combine or agree to prevent wages from going up or even to lower them.

Let us submit each of these explanations to analysis.

(a) If the first reason were true, the employers with more economic resources would pay lower wages and those who are less well-off, higher ones. Observation reveals that it is the opposite that takes place, and numerous statistics, unnecessary to quote, show that it is the larger concerns that pay higher wages and establish better working conditions. More generally, if it were true that the price of a good depended on the relative capacity of buyers and sellers to wait, bread would be permanently overpriced, since the buyers are pressed to consume it, while the sellers, who, generally speaking, have larger resources than most of the consumers, could wait calmly until the sellers bid among themselves and raised its price to a level at which the bakers of bread would deign to sell.

Besides, it is not correct to say that the workers have absolutely no reserves and that they cannot afford to wait. The proof of this lies in the fact that they do wait. Lastly, a waiting period can also be ruinous for capitalists and entrepreneurs, since they will suffer a loss if they do not employ the factors at their disposal. The answer that they could hire other workers would not be valid, because a rebuttal would be in order to the effect that the workers can proceed in the same way and direct themselves to other persons who demand their services.

(b) The idea that work is a perishable good is even less tenable. The answer was given, a long time ago, that so is interest and that the owner of capital who does not invest it loses the income it could yield as surely as the man who is out of work loses his salary. In the second place, and going to the bottom of the argument, the idea is itself defective. Withholding work would not diminish its supply but simply delay it. At a given moment fewer people would offer their services, but the number would be proportionally larger later on.

(c) With respect to employers' agreements for the purpose

of lowering wages, it is sometimes said that they are tacit, since they are not seen competing for the available labor force. On other occasions it is asserted that this agreement is achieved through associations which pursue the same objective. The first argument reproduces the popular error of believing that competition is present solely when one of the competing parties makes visible efforts to prevent his rivals from obtaining something that he desires as well. Against this point of view, it must be affirmed that competition exists by virtue of the fact that someone is willing to buy. Competition will be real and unrestricted so long as those interested in buying can purchase what they desire at prevailing prices.

As for employers' cartels, let us suppose that they came into being. In that case, each employer would keep for himself the difference between the wage rate which should be in force as a result of the marginal productivity of labor and the monopoly rate that he would be able to impose. To this effect it would be necessary that employers should also agree, in their capacity as sellers of the articles that they produce, not to dispose of the articles at reduced prices in spite of their lower cost. If this were not done, the gain would be passed on to the consumers. In other words, a universal monopoly of all productive activities would be required, which would be possible only through institutional restrictions that would convert entrepreneurs into a closed class.

We can carry our refutation a step farther and call attention to the fact that this pretended monopolistic combination by employers would be a demand monopoly, that is, a monopsony; that demand monopolies are really supply monopolies of a special nature; that in order for them to succeed, it is necessary for entrepreneurs to control a factor necessary for every kind of production; and that since this factor does not exist, entrepreneurs would have to monopolize all material productive factors, a situation which can be achieved only by a socialist community.

Neither would the owners of the material factors of production be able to organize a gigantic cartel against the interest of the workers. The fact that the scarcity of labor is greater than the scarcity of primary factors would prevent it. In other words, throughout the world there is land that is not sown and minerals that are not extracted, and this is so because the comparatively greater scarcity of labor determines the degree to which the comparatively more abundant natural factors are exploited. An agreement among the owners of the resources presently being used for production would not be sufficient. It would be indispensable to have the owners of all land and resources, without exception, participate in such a cartel. Otherwise, production could be begun from submarginal land and the competition from that production would be enough to cause a cartel which did not include the owners of that land to fail. It is obvious that these assumptions cannot be realized in practice. Therefore, a monopoly of the demand for labor does not and cannot exist in a free economy.

If the causes that can engender an exploitation of labor are inoperative, as I believe I have shown, it is impossible to affirm the existence of such exploitation as a general proposition. The worker would be exploited if he were paid a wage below his marginal productivity. The idea that this takes place in reality is as untenable as the notion that in a free market prices are chronically too low.

Nothing in what I have written should be understood as meaning that cases of exploitation cannot or do not exist in fact. This will take place when a group of workers compete among themselves and are faced by a monopolistic employer. But the immense majority of writers agree that this occurrence is infrequent, temporary, local, and not important. It is due (and this is merely another way of saying that the market for labor is imperfect and of pointing out the causes that make it so) to (1) lack of information on the part of the workers with regard to other opportunities for work; (2) lack of mobility, arising from want of the resources needed to transfer to some other place, or from circumstances which tie a man down to a certain place, such as the possession of a home or family reasons; (3) specialization that prevents a worker from changing to some other occupation. These limitations are to be regretted, and everything possible should be done in order to make them disappear, both in general and in concrete cases. On the one hand, it is necessary to attack the monopolistic positions of employers and to try to eliminate them; on the other, efforts should be made to favor the utmost mobility of workers and to undertake other justified measures which it would be out of place to study here.

As may be seen, it is not freedom or competition that prevents a laborer from receiving the normal wage rate. On the contrary, it is precisely the absence of freedom and competition, and their failure to function fully in some instances, that result in a worker not collecting his full compensation according to the data of the market. Once more it is apparent that the idea that exploitation constitutes the ordinary situation and is due to alleged inferiorities on the part of workmen, is absolutely false. As Hutt, one of the specialists who has shed much light on this problem, says: "It is quite true that the poorer a workman is, the higher will be the marginal utility to him of further increments of income, that is, of those commodities in general which satisfy his needs; but whilst it is clear that this will affect the intensity or amount of his efforts to get further income, we have no reason at all to suppose that it will (a) prevent in any way the formation of an effective market for his labor, (b) cause an equilibrium in the market at a lower rate than would result from the same quantity of labor being offered by workers to whom the marginal utilities of income were lower."[9]

The Goals of Pro-Labor, Pro-Union Policies

Having cleared the way by removing the obstacles opposed by the theories that I have examined, we can proceed to the principal object of this investigation. For this purpose I deem

[9]Hutt, W. H., *The Theory of Collective Bargaining.* P. S. King and Son, Ltd., London, 1930, p. 64.

11

it convenient to state in a more precise way the goals pursued by labor legislation and the means to which it has resorted in order to attain these goals.

The overriding end of labor policy is to secure greater well-being for this part of the community, in the first place of a material nature. Governments, labor unions, and workers individually strive to obtain:

An increased remuneration.

More free time, that is, shorter working hours, more rest periods, longer vacations, etc.

Better working conditions from the viewpoints of physical safety, health, comfort, etc.

More economic security.

The Means Employed

These objectives are pursued (a) through the action of the government and (b) through the action of labor unions. The first-named can put into effect certain formal determinations, such as a law on the duration of the working day, a regulation on measures to prevent accidents, a resolution to establish a minimum wage, or the decision of an arbitrator or of a labor court settling a dispute. It may also be content to rely on persuasion and on the government's influence. But in the last resort we always find the possibility of the application of coercion or of the use of force which is characteristic of all official action.

Action by the workers is almost solely collective and presupposes unionization, that is, the enrollment of workmen in professional groups. The two chief means it employs are collective bargaining and strikes, which we can compare with treaties and wars in the international sphere.

Are these two distinct and separate worlds, and do they operate independently? Although it is conceivable that this could happen, things do not take place in this way. I do not refer to the goals, which I have already said are identical, nor to the political connections of trade unions with parties and governments. Neither do I consider it of importance to remark that the number of workers who belong to the unions is directly proportional to the stimulus and even to the pressure exerted by public authorities. *What I have in mind is that the effectiveness of labor action depends as well and in the last resort on the government in the sense that such action would be nugatory were it not for the complacency or support of the government.* This is not a criticism, merely an analysis of facts and explanation of the reality of the situation. In the final analysis, the action exerted by workers is based on coercion and violence, just as government measures are.

If labor unions were truly organizations for the purpose of bargaining collectively with respect to wages, their efforts would not be capable of raising them above the level determined by an unhampered market, except in the infrequent cases of exploitation to which I referred above. This is the consequence of the fact which we verified that wage rates are not the result of the "strength" or "weakness" of the parties to the labor contract, but of the supply of and the demand for labor, and therefore of its marginal utility. From a catallactic point of view, collective bargaining would not differ from individual bargaining. In contradiction to this, we observe every day that labor demands and the discussion of collective agreements secure "good results" for the members of the union that takes part in them. The explanation is that what is involved in such cases is not a free bargain, but a forced one, based on discussions which have as a background the threat of a strike or, in some countries, of a strike first and then of a settlement dictated by the government.

In the majority of countries, at the present time, a strike is not a mere suspension of work by those workmen who do not find the conditions offered by employers to their liking. It is a suspension accompanied by violence for the purpose of preventing nonstriking workers from working and of keeping away those new men who would enroll for work because these conditions constitute a gain in comparison with those conditions in effect where they have been rendering their services. Violence is sometimes exerted by the workers themselves, as is the case in the United States. In other countries, violence is exerted by public authorities, as happens in Mexico.

It is true that in the great nation to our north the principle that workers can paralyze the operation of the organization that employs them and even close it down, has not been recognized, or rather, has not been acknowledged officially. On the contrary, the Taft-Hartley Act prescribes expressly that every employee has the right to work in spite of a strike and forbids threats and acts of violence. The decisions of law courts are to the same effect. As a matter of fact, however, according to reports of reliable observers, labor unions have acquired the privilege of employing violence and they practice it with some impunity. Labor unions prevent access to industrial plants by force and they ill-treat and injure those who dare to challenge them. As a rule, police do not hinder the unions, or they interfere ineffectively. The public attorneys do not prosecute the guilty parties; and courts are deprived of the opportunity of punishing them.

In other countries, as in Mexico, the situation is even worse. Although the Constitution limits itself to admitting the right to strike, forbids violent acts against persons or property, and guarantees that every man shall be free to engage in the profession, industry, trade, or endeavor that is agreeable to him as long as it is licit, a law enacted in 1925 declared that the person who attempts to work in an enterprise where the majority of workers have declared a strike offends the rights of society.[10] This is not the place to undertake a study of such restriction from the viewpoint of constitutional law, although, in my opinion, it limits the right to work to such an extent that it becomes illusory. What seems more important is to underline the fact that in order to prevent their employer from turning elsewhere for his labor force, the strikers are compelled to keep their fellow employees, as well as any person

[10]An Act to Regulate Article 4 of the Constitution in the Part that Refers to Freedom to Work, December 18, 1925. This law was the precedent for Articles 7 and 8 of the Federal Labor Law.

willing and able to work, from having access to the employer and to his plant and idle installations. In other words, the truth is that the suspension of work is not directed against the management, but against those workers who do not accept the strike. Of course, it harms the owners of the plant but primarily and to a much deeper degree it hurts the rest of the working class. For the latter, the wages and other working conditions that the employer offers and that the strikers reject, represent an advantageous alternative when compared with the lower salaries and less favorable terms that they will be forced to accept if the other offers are foreclosed to them. The only reason why they do not accept the more advantageous offers is the existence of a legal prohibition, enforced by the threat of a penalty and the power of the government.

To say, as someone has done, that in Mexico, public power is at the service of the right of strikers not to work, in opposition to the property rights of employers, constitutes an inadmissible simplification. The truth is that force has been put at the disposal of privileged minority groups (the men who strike in a factory or even in a complete industry are usually a minority when compared to all possible workers), in opposition to the majority of the working population and to the detriment of its interests. *The right which contemporary monopolistic labor unions invoke and of which they boast is not a right not to work, because nobody denies them this. It is a right to prevent others from working through coercion and force.* It is as unjustified and as absurd as if a group of former Catholics claimed the right to abandon the Catholic Church and not to profess this religion as a valid reason for the public authorities to prevent those who were still loyal to Rome from entering Catholic Churches and from worshipping there.

The Specific Objectives of Unions

I pointed out above that both official and labor union action seek more well-being for workers in the several respects that I enumerated. Now that we have studied the true character of the means, or, speaking more precisely of the political means, in the strict sense of the word, that are employed for this purpose, we can also specify the concrete objectives that are pursued. In the case of salaries, the purpose is to force the employer to fix a wage rate above that of a free market. Substantially the same thing takes place with regard to the length of the working day which does not increase the entrepreneur's cost, but does diminish the return that he receives in exchange for it. (In the case of excessive working hours, it is possible that a diminution in the span of the work-day may result in greater productivity). The betterment of the other conditions of workers, in respect to safety, health, and similar matters already mentioned, likewise results in larger expenditures. Generally speaking, the conclusions that we reach in the case of salaries will also apply to such improvements in working conditions as are introduced. Technically, therefore, what we are confronted with in such cases is not different from other instances of government intervention, that is, cases in which the state makes use of its apparatus and power to modify the results that the operation of a free market would produce in the matter of prices (as in the case of salaries) or in order to limit production (as in the case of a reduction of the time devoted to work).

The Effects of Interventionist Measures

I have studied elsewhere the results produced by interventionist measures. It would therefore be sufficient if I repeated the reasoning and conclusions included in the article to which I refer. But since they were presented there in an abridged fashion, owing to the fact that it was originally written for a business review,[11] and since I believe that it may be fruitful to go deeper in the examination of this species of intervention-

[11]Velasco, G. R., "The Greatest Danger, the State." Published in English as "Intervention Leads to Total Control," in *The Freeman* for January, 1970, Irvington-on-Hudson, New York.

ism, I shall attempt a detailed demonstration of the effects that are to be expected when one follows the Webbs' advice and when workers are protected from the effects of competition and of the other forces which operate in an unhampered market.

The case which 'traditional laborites' believe it is easiest to defend is that of minimum wages. (I designate them 'traditional laborites' in order to distinguish myself from them, since I have proclaimed that I am for whatever favors the workers.) Who can object to a man receiving at least five dollars daily, let us say? Who can declare himself against any human being's having enough for a decent existence, even a very modest one, especially if he is married and his children are to grow up healthy and be useful to their country?

And yet it is impossible to make a man worth a certain sum of money by decreeing that it will be against the law for any person to offer him a lesser amount. To begin with, if such a method were suitable, why should we not end this man's poverty and decide that he will receive ten, twenty, fifty dollars a day? The truth is that the law cannot, without causing serious disturbances, force employers to pay a wage above the value of their marginal product. Naturally, if the minimum wage is set at the point where all those who seek employment will find it, no economic effects will be produced. But if the wage is fixed at a higher level, the only result will be that some men will be unable to find work. This happens because the primary function of prices is to clear the market, that is, to insure that all those who are willing to sell at the equilibrium price are able to do so, and that all those desirous of buying at that same price will do so, with the consequence that no supply and no demand remain unsatisfied. Instead, if the price fixed by law is higher than the equilibrium rate, a part of the supply will not be absorbed, just as part of the demand will not be filled if the price is lower than it should be.

The sad fact is that there are some individuals who are so ignorant or so clumsy or so inefficient or so irresponsible (including many who are not to blame, whose intelligence is subnormal or who are ailing or invalid) that they are unable at a given moment to earn even the wage paid to unskilled workmen who occupy the lowest rung in the scale of labor. If, despite this fact, for which no one is responsible, and contrary to the teaching of economic science, it is decreed that such men will be forbidden to offer their services except at the rates approved by social reformers, the only effect will be to deprive them of the possibility of finding any gainful employment and the community of receiving even the modest contribution which their condition permits them to render. The fact is that they are turned into economic outcasts. The doors of industry and of all other activities where it is possible to enforce compliance with the laws on minimum wages are closed to them. Thus, they are forced to look for employment in agriculture, in that great sponge which in Mexico and other countries soaks up the unemployed, or to seek refuge in lines of work which hardly merit the name, as in itinerant selling, shoe-shining, and garbage collecting, or in begging and delinquency.

The essential point to be grasped is that if the laws on minimum wages succeed in raising wages, they will almost inevitably cause submarginal workers to lose their jobs. The resulting damage for the poorest and most helpless part of society will be in proportion to the discrepancy between the wage rates fixed by law and those determined by a free market. The individuals condemned to die from hunger or to subsist on public charity will be similarly more or less numerous.

Actually, there is another possibility which has not occurred in fact, owing to the belief that minimum wages can produce only beneficient results. It consists in adopting this measure with full knowledge of the consequences that it will bring with it, and in providing whatever is necessary so that a community will care for those it prevents from earning their own living. It is obvious that only an affluent society will be in a position to do this, a society in which total production will be so high as to provide the necessary amounts for supporting those sections of the population who are capable of earning only the wages that cannot be tolerated. If this responsibility is not assumed, we will have to agree with an author who writes that "what labor sadly needs is protection against its 'friends'!"[12]

Similar considerations apply in the case of any other salaries which are set at levels above those determined by an unhampered market, through labor-union pressure or by a decision of the government. Strictly speaking, these are not true wages, but rather decrees, orders issued by the government or by other official organizations, because from an economic point of view there are no prices except those formed in a market. In full agreement with advocates of a pro-labor policy, I want the income of workers to be as high as possible. However, I have no alternative but to concur with the American Federation of Labor, when it declares that "living standards do not rise by any magic formula. They can rise only when workers produce more per hour and per year of work."[13] Or, to repeat the opinion of the Government of the United States, as expressed in an official publication, that "the material well-being of a people and especially of ordinary workers who make up the masses of the population cannot rise above the efficiency of a nation's economy and the volume of production available for domestic consumption."[14]

The General Theory of Wages

Before proceeding to demonstrate this proposition, which is accepted by practically all economists, it may be useful to recall some of the conclusions reached by the theory of wages. In this way we shall lay the bases for correctly appraising dominant tendencies and for understanding why they yield the results which I am about to describe.

[12]King, Wilford I., *The Keys to Prosperity*, Constitution and Free Enterprise Foundation, New York, 1948, p. 213.

[13]Quoted by Jules Backman in *Wages and Prices*, The Foundation for Economic Education, Irvington-on-Hudson, 1947, p. 48.

[14]*The Gift of Freedom*, United States Department of Labor, Bureau of Labor Statistics, p. 9.

Except in the case of personal services such as those provided by a servant or a chauffeur, the demand for labor is a derived demand. This means that the employer is a middleman between those who sell their services and those who consume goods, an intermediary who buys those services in order to resell them incorporated in what he produces. The idea that entrepreneurs employ workers and fix wages and working conditions at their own pleasure, even freely, is thus seen to be false. In fact, it is the consumers who ultimately employ workers and who decide what compensation and other terms they are to enjoy. It is the consumers, as economists insist, who really pay wages. Slichter, one of the writers who has devoted much time to studying labor problems, goes so far as to assert that when bargaining with regard to the terms of collective agreements, "management, of course, represents the interests of consumers."[15] Consequently, a price is assigned to a man's work and that price has to be the one that prevails in the market, not because entrepreneurs are sensible and soulless men, but because they are subject in their turn to the wishes and dictates of consumers. Thus, we see that a businessman can continue to pay wages only as long as he finds buyers for the goods or services that he provides, at a price sufficient to meet what he disburses in salaries, plus all his other costs. Among these, labor constitutes a cost factor which varies from one case to another, but which forms the greatest one by far. In the United States it has been estimated that payments for personal services represent from 60% to 80% of the national income, according to how they are defined.

If these findings are correct, from an economic standpoint, there is no basis for that unsurmountable opposition, for that antagonism which the Marxist ideology prevailing today (and prevailing in some circles that believe themselves to be most opposed to it) postulates as a starting point for the exhortations with which it seeks to set one class of society against

[15]Slichter, Sumner, *The Challenge of Industrial Relations*, Cornell University Press, Ithaca, 1947, p. 30.

another. (In passing, may I mention the fallacy of speaking about social "classes" in a community governed by the principles of a free economy.) Capital and labor are not competitors, much less enemies, but instead co-operant factors of production. Besides, since workers make up in numbers almost the totality of consumers, the prejudice that they work for the benefit of other people turns out to be completely unfounded. It is not a play on words but the strictest truth to answer that in any economy devoted to mass production, workers labor for their own benefit, with the cooperation of the owners of natural resources and of capital. The entrepreneurs coordinate labor and capital, to whom both submit equally, so that the entrepreneurs may organize and direct them, and most importantly, can assume the vital social function of undertaking the risks of production. In the process that I describe, besides not having to run those risks, each productive agent receives in exchange for his contribution a price which tends to equal the value of the marginal product of the total supply of that factor. Returning indirectly to the subject of exploitation, through this system of production, which is as well and simultaneously a system of distribution, we find each person is compensated in accordance with his contribution, whether it consists of labor, capital, or natural resources.

The market, which constitutes the heart of the system, is at the same time a mechanism which fixes prices and which governs production. Each of these functions is as essential as the other, although the governing of production is especially far-reaching for the workers, owing to the fact that capitalists, owners, and entrepreneurs are no more than a small minority. But let us consider a little more leisurely the first role of the market, that of price-setter for the services of each factor of production and therefore of allotter of the social income. In the first place, I call attention to the fact that the procedure followed in order to value the contribution of each agent is exactly the same and that the determination of wages does not take place in a different way from that of interest or of rents. Even entrepreneurial profits offer certain differences insofar as they are a residual element, that is, what is left of the price after deducting the payments made to the other factors. Such profits can be considered, as Frank Knight, one of the most highly regarded American economists, does, as the payment of a service; namely, that of responsible direction.[16] In the second place, I insist that modern theory, after rejecting other explanations such as the subsistency theory (with its demagogic variant of the notorious "iron law"), that of historical and and social forces, and of the wage fund, has agreed that what determines the value of labor is its marginal productivity. This means that wage rates depend finally on the value that the wage earner's fellow men ascribe to his services and achievement.

In order to forestall an objection which my exposition is certain to raise, I admit beforehand that although the principle of marginal productivity possesses an undoubted theoretical validity, in the actual world it operates as a force or tendency, for which reason it is possible that at a given moment the wage of an individual worker may not equal the value of his marginal product. The labor market, like all other markets, indeed like all human institutions, is imperfect and that reality may exhibit extensive deviations from the normal wage rates, especially in cases where the buyer of personal services has attained a monopolistic position and where workers are lacking in the information or the resources necessary to put an end to this situation. However, one should not believe that the imperfections in the labor market rebound in all cases to the damage of wage earners. Contemporary thought is of the opinion that "it is not so certain that actual wages in the wider labor market are below normal rates most of the time. It seems rather to be true that wage adjustments lag behind the influences which tend to pull the price of labor upward or downward, so that market rates are somewhat below their normals in periods of rising prices or of increasing

[16]Knight, Frank, "The Determination of Just Wages," mimeographed copy, p. 30.

demand for labor, and above them in periods of falling prices or of decreasing demand."[17]

Under the other aspect that I pointed out, the function of a free market consists in inducing producers to provide those things which consumers want, so as to achieve the fullest possible satisfaction of human needs. In the specific case of labor, when wage rates are formed freely in view of supply and demand, their purpose is to guide workers toward those sectors of economic activity in which the wants of consumers manifest themselves most intensely. As a result of this, fluctuations in wage rates are the means used by an economy in order for the sovereignty of consumers to assert itself in the labor market. Through such fluctuations, the available amount of the labor force is distributed among the different branches of production. And the appropriate rate in any zone or in any class of occupation will be the one that calls forth the needed supply of labor, comparatively to other opportunities for its utilization.

The Effects of Above-Market Wage Rates

Although this excursion in the field of theory has turned out rather long, it will probably shorten our inquiry into the consequences that are to be expected of overraised wages, that is, of those which labor unions succeed in imposing above market rates, through the threat of a strike or through a formal resolution or constraint by the government. The answer provided by economists is direct and unmistakable. "It is a well-known generalization of theoretical economics that a wage which is held above the equilibrium level necessarily involves unemployment and a diminution of the value of capital."[18] To this quotation from Robbins, I could add as many as can be desired, both from works of a general character, as from

[17]Bye, Raymond T., *Principles of Economics*, F. S. Crofts & Co., New York, 1947, p. 498.
[18]Robbins, Lionel, *An Essay on the Nature and Significance of Economic Science*, Macmillan and Co., London, 1935, p. 146.

23

those dealing especially with salaries, by Cannan, Hutt, Benham, Bye, Mises, Fairchild, Hicks, Dobb, Simons, Machlup
. . . It is easy to find the explanation for this unanimity of
opinions. "This is one of the most elementary deductions from
the theory of economic equilibrium," as the above-mentioned
Robbins adds. Whenever a price is set at a level higher than
that which the market would have determined if it had been
left alone, the balance between supply and demand is altered.
In that case there will exist potential sellers, in this instance
the workers, who will be unable to sell, that is, to find employment, because there will be no buyers, no one to make a contract for their services. A part of the labor supply will remain
unabsorbed by productive activities. In a word, the result
will be unemployment.

In view of the importance of this conclusion and the possibility of certain variations, it will be worth our while to
examine in more detail what happens when wages are raised
artificially by force. For this purpose we must distinguish the
situation in which wage fixing is only partial from that which
is created when the majority of firms and industries have been
withdrawn from a regime of free competition. In the former
hypothesis, the demand for labor will certainly decrease in
the plants or sector where wages are controlled. Entrepreneurs
will lay off part of their personnel immediately or as soon as
they are able to do so. Simultaneously, they will abstain from
increasing their labor force or will even study permanent ways
of replacing it or of reducing it through the introduction of
more machinery, of new or more efficient equipment, or
through the adoption of other procedures. As regards new
industries, the rise in the cost of the labor factor will operate
in the direction of postponing or altering the projects for
them. As a result of all this, a certain number of men who
would have had or would have found work in the activities
where wages are overraised, will not have employment or will
have to look for it elsewhere. A redistribution of the labor
force will be effected, as a result of which the sector with
controlled industries will have a lesser number of workers

than what it could have employed. In the remaining economic activities more labor will be offered. The necessary corollary of this movement, and of the more plentiful supply of workers who compete among themselves for a smaller number of jobs, will be to depress the salary rates that prevailed formerly in those activities. It is undeniable that the workmen favored by the rise will be better off (save for the damage that they will suffer as consumers, together with all other users of the article which they manufacture), but the improvement in their conditions will have been secured in exchange for worsening those of their fellows who have been dismissed or deprived of the opportunity to obtain employment and of the working class in general.

It might therefore seem that the remedy lies in extending the blessings of wage control to industry as a whole (instead of just the ones where a strike occurred or to which a decision by the labor courts applies) or even to all business and to all economic activity. In this way it would appear to be impossible for the injurious effects which I have explained to take place anywhere. Nothing could be more superficial or more deceptive. If industries capable of absorbing the unemployed (both those actually dismissed and all those to whom over-raised wages closed the doors of factories) are no longer in existence, then the lack of employment will be not merely temporary, but permanent. That is, it will have to persist indefinitely until the economic forces which in the long run determine the height of wages (capital accumulation, inventions and new technological processes, the movements of foreign trade) bring about such a change in the wages that would have been paid in a competitive market as to make it possible to absorb the unemployed. One should go further and designate this form of unemployment by the name which belongs to it, that of institutional unemployment, in order to stress that it is not a product of economic phenomena, but of motivations and decisions of a different character. This institutional unemployment will not disappear as long as the government or the unions are successful in maintaining artificial wage rates or as long as they do not modify them. It is also possible that it will be absorbed by virtue of more general and profound causes, especially in the long run. But the conclusions at which we have arrived remain valid. Every rise in wages above the level of a free market causes unemployment. "When unionism was restricted to skilled labor mainly," writes Mises, with the terseness and vigor which have made him the upholder of the illustrious tradition of the Austrian School of Economics, "the wage rise achieved by the unions did not lead to institutional unemployment. It merely lowered the height of wage rates in those branches in which there were no efficient unions or no unions at all."[19] On the contrary, when labor unions or government action in the matter of salaries extend to the whole economy or even to the main part of it, the only result is unemployment, not local but general; not accidental but normal; not transitory but chronic. The unemployment of millions of human beings which we witnessed in Great Britain and the United States until the coming of the Second World War made it possible to conceal the consequence of this policy which supposedly favors the classes without property, i.e., the unemployment characteristic of this age of laborism or unionism.

The unemployment from which we suffer in Mexico belongs to the other variety. Although less visible and serious, its existence is undeniable, and its characteristics are precisely those foreseen and described by theory. Side by side with workmen who each time receive more for exerting themselves less and in more comfortable conditions, an enormous mass is excluded by "prolabor" policy from the better sort of occupations and condemned to live in poverty. Whoever does not perceive this should read the accounts about the situation in England from 1850 to 1890, which offers surprising points of resemblance to our present state. There a labor aristocracy had also come into existence which went so far as to declare openly that excluded workers made up a morally inferior class,

[19]Mises, Ludwig von, *Human Action*, Yale University Press, New Haven, 1949, p. 764.

incapable of rising through its own efforts. Against this depressed class the employed workers believed they were forced to protect themselves through unionization and overraised wages, because otherwise they would be pulled down to the same level. If a historical comparison of this kind is not sufficient to convince a proponent of laborism of its futility, he would be well advised to leave the cities, where we find the factories of which we are so proud in our endeavor to industrialize our country, with their brand-new equipment, their dining rooms for the workers, and their social services, and to visit the smaller towns and the rural villages of Mexico. In this way he can see for himself whether we have not been creating two classes, one of them comparatively well-off (because the inflation that we have undergone has probably harmed it less than all others, if we except some entrepreneurs), and the other one destitute of everything, and what is worse, without hope of deliverance as long as predominant ideas do not change and their consequence is not modified.

I must return to a theoretical analysis before I am accused of becoming sentimental or of turning to demagoguery. In the words of Ortega y Gasset, I shall reply that "I have not come here to discuss politics and even if I had, it would not be a sentimental brand of politics."[20] My purpose is precisely to bring to this vital debate over the way of improving the conditions of our proletarian masses, the teachings of economics, which is equivalent to saying, that of reason in opposition to sentiment. Incidentally, I shall remark that what differentiates social reformers are not the lofty aims which they pretend to monopolize, nor their greater philanthropy. As Hazlitt has pointed out, their real characteristic is their greater impatience and, I would add, their shortsightendess, in its turn due to their failure to take economic science into account. Besides the fact that the arguments they put forth are always sentimental and sensational and that their best proposals are such as to solve only today's problem, at best, they seem unable to

[20]Ortega y Gasset, José "Mision de la Universidad" (*"The Task of a University"*), Revista de Occidente, Madrid, 1930, p. 25.

comprehend the consequences that will supervene inevitably, as in the case of wages, as soon as we look beyond the immediate foreground. One is even tempted to believe that they do not worry about such questions and that their motto is the well-known saying of Louis XV and his mistress Dubarry: *Aprés nous le déluge!* Concerning the above-mentioned question of wages, Hazlitt continues "the apparently easy method of raising them by government fiat is the wrong way and the worst way . . . The best way" and I shall again venture to collaborate with this distinguished opponent of economic fallacies, by pointing out that it is the only way, "to raise wages, therefore, is to raise labor productivity."[21]

[21]Hazlitt, *op. cit.*, p. 142.

Chapter II

Some Objections Considered

IT SEEMS ALMOST UNNECESSARY TO REMARK THAT THE THESIS I have presented has not gone uncontested. Thus, an account which is widespread among labor leaders maintains that the evils I have pointed out are imaginary because wage increases are, in fact, obtained at the expense of employers, whose profits are thereby reduced to a fair or reasonable level. Before analyzing this comforting belief, it may be useful to inquire into its probable origins. It appears to rest on the habit of regarding "capital" and "labor" as competing elements that vie with each other for the income that derives from production and on the simple idea that when wage rates are raised, the whole working population has to benefit thereby. I have already refuted the first view, and I wish merely to add on this occasion that the common assumption that when two interests are in opposition, what is bad for one of them must necessarily be good for the other, is clearly untenable. It may well happen, as it does in the present instance, that the act under discussion is harmful for both of them. As for the second argument advanced in support of the theory that I am going to examine, it forgets that it is perfectly possible that with higher wage rates, we may have a smaller total wage income. This will occur whenever the volume of employment diminishes by a greater percentage than the increase in the wage rate. In that case, even if the multiplier (in the purely arithmetical sense of the word and therefore without any Keynesian overtones) is larger, since the multiplicand is smaller, the product will also be less, namely, the income obtained by the working class as a whole.

But let us see why this idea that wages raised above their free-market height can be taken out of the pockets of employers without further trouble is mistaken. (Incidentally, please notice that in this sort of discussion, entrepreneurs or employers are always regarded as "rich men," and it is always assumed that they are bound to make profits, in complete disregard of the very high mortality of business concerns.) If the demand for the product of the firm in which the rise in wages takes place is relatively inelastic, the producer will pass the higher cost on to the consumers in the form of higher prices. We have such evident and recent examples of this in Mexico that I consider it unnecessary to amplify this comment. I limit myself to pointing out that it will be the consumers who will be exploited if this happens, among them the workers, who will see their real wages shrink. But let us suppose that this first way of defending himself is closed to the entrepreneur because circumstances will not permit prices to go up (for example, because we are dealing with a public utility, and the competent authorities will not allow a change in the rates, or for any other reason). In this case, the increase in wages must come out of profits. But this will not avoid such unfavorable results as partial unemployment, accompanied by the reduction of wages in activities that are not under government control, or even general and permanent unemployment. Besides, it is an illusion to believe that capital will accept being exploited for an indefinite length of time. It is obvious that new capital will refuse to invest for the expansion of existing plants or for the establishment of new enterprises of the nature of those affected by the increase in wages. As regards the owners of the capital that cannot turn to other lines, they will invest what is strictly necessary in order that their concern may continue to operate and yield a return, but they will not try to replace the machines and equipment that wear out or become obsolete. All their efforts will aim at closing the business as rapidly as they can, selling out and recovering as much as possible on their investment. They will invest in other branches of production or, if necessary, in other countries, and in the last resort will prefer not to invest, but to use their funds for consumption.

Our conclusion must be that "no factor of production can maintain the cooperation of another factor by offering it or leaving it an amount of the product less than the value of the net product elsewhere . . . Hence, we can say that monopoly gains by any factor are ultimately obtained by exploiting the consumer, although incidental losses are usually thrown upon other co-operant factors."[22] And since all the workingmen are consumers, the benefits that they apparently achieve at the expense of the other factors result for them in a proportionally higher real loss. The belief that the entrepreneur is the only one harmed when wages exceed the rates that a free market would set, turns out to be not only false but a tragic deception and a mockery.

Economic science asserts that between the phenomena that it studies there exist inexorable regularities of succession and interconnection. In the last resort, therefore, economic laws do not differ from natural laws. Only one way is open in order to escape from their action: to modify the conditions that are necessary for their operation. Thus, the main task of applied economics, once ethics and politics determine the goals at which one should aim, is to create the conditions required so that the laws which will produce the desired results will function, to suppress the conditions which will cause those laws not to function or which will bring into play other laws that would produce the opposite results.

But the inalterable character to which I refer (and which cannot be denied unless we also deny the existence of a science

---

[22]Hutt, W. H., *op. cit.*, p. 95.

of economics), should not lead us to forget that the operation of economic laws is far from being invested with the exactness or the spectacular nature of physical laws. This is not due to their being less certain or to the fact of their enjoying a limited validity, but purely and simply to the immensely greater complexity of human actions, particularly when they take place within the framework of society. To express this by a way of a comparison, in the field of mechanics we find simple causes and simple effects, which are fully and unequivocally determinable in reality and which are capable of being measured or estimated quantitatively. In the matter of wages, on the contrary, a given cause (for instance, a certain increase) will not act alone but accompanied by a multiplicity of other causes, whether prior, simultaneous or later, with the consequence that the results will be correspondingly complex and that prediction will not be possible except within ample margins and much less capable of quantitative measurement or estimation. In other words, in economics constant relations do not exist. It is not possible to announce the precise effect of any action, even if all the original data are known exactly and all other conditions continue to be the same. But from this limitation, it does not follow that economic laws can be suspended or transgressed with impunity. To repeat, the regularities which they describe are inevitable. If the facts that they presuppose are present, the consequences that correspond to them will occur necessarily.

If I take the liberty of recalling these truths with which you are well acquainted, it is in order to be able to answer another objection to my thesis. It will not fail to be said that in the real world, not in that of the lucubrations in which I have allowed myself the pleasure of indulging, things take place in a very different manner. Everyday wages are raised in factories as a result of strikes or in order to prevent them, and nevertheless not a worker is dismissed. The unemployment that I gloomily prophesy is nowhere to be seen. On the contrary, it may even happen that more jobs are offered in the establishments concerned, thus proving that the other prediction of my dismal science is equally untrue.

32

It would be naive to think that any science worthy of the name would have failed to take into account such obvious objections. Moreover, they are not peculiar to the subject of labor but the kind of objections that are always made by those who do not understand the nature of economic theory and who think that the events it announces must follow with the punctuality of the eclipses foretold by astronomers or as visibly as the reactions expected by chemistry. The only difference in this case is the care with which writers have enumerated the various kinds of circumstances whose presence will determine that things will not develop in the way I have described or that will hide from the eyes of those lacking in knowledge the connection between the rise in wages and the unemployment that constitutes its catallactic consequence.

To begin with, this may happen, as in the case when an industry is in a position to pass the increased cost on to the consumers without suffering a reduction in demand, in spite of the higher prices. The effect on the number of workers employed will depend on the possibility of conserving the market, which can even increase as a result of other causes. We thus have a first example in which the workers will have obtained more pay for their efforts without having to undergo any decrease in their number or with a reduction that will not be in proportion to the number employed. In any event, as Machlup has noted, even in those industries with relatively elastic demand, a certain period of time has to elapse before the effects of a rise in wages display themselves.[23] The rise in prices may be delayed, or the market may not react immediately to it, or the firm may not act right away in spite of the drop in new orders. When it does finally decide to do without some of the men, it is possible that machinery will be installed to do their work. In this case the situation will become even more confused, and the workers will blame the new equipment for their dismissal instead of the real reason, the increase

[23]Machlup, F., "Monopolistic Wage Determination as a Part of the General Problem of Monopoly," in *Wage Determination and the Economics of Liberalism*, Chamber of Commerce of the United States, Washington, 1947, pp. 51–52.

in wages. This was why capital was invested in machines instead of being devoted to other uses.

On a third hypothesis, the general tendency can be so favorable to a certain industry that in spite of difficulties such as those originated by the greater outlay for personal services, its progress will not be stopped, and it will even employ more men than before. This is the case of those lines which exploit new inventions or technical advances, such as artificial fibers or plastics in the last few years, or electronics and apparatus for space exploration and travel in the United States.

Another element which will tend to hide the harm caused by artificially raised wage rates is to be found in monetary or banking policy. If the economic process that prevails is one of inflation or credit expansion, demand will be stimulated by the greater abundance of means of payment and will not decrease, with the result that the level of employment will not decline. Finally, even when no real reasons like those enumerated are present, people will not be lacking who will invent other reasons, in more or less good faith and as I have pointed out, that the complexity of economic phenomena makes it difficult to perceive their causation and relations. Thus, the unemployment that existed in the United States from 1930 to 1940 was successively attributed to the fact that the dollar was overvalued, to the stagnation of a mature economy, to underconsumption, to an excess of savings, and to all sorts of other farfetched causes, although the real, effective one was at hand for all to see.

It is impossible to get away from the dilemma: either real wage rates, determined in a free market, with full employment and a maximum total income for personal services; or falsified wage rates, imposed by coercion on the part of the government or labor unions, with unemployment and a smaller total income for personal services. As Mises puts it, the problem consists in deciding "whether there is any means for raising the standard of living of all those eager to work other than raising the marginal productivity of labor by accelerating the increase of capital as compared with population."[24] In the words of

[24]Mises, *op. cit.*, p. 766.

Hutt, the answer must be that "every insistence on an artificially high rate will tend to reduce the number it will be
profitable to employ. Those within the combination will still
benefit at the expense of those outside. This method of obtaining monopoly is more pernicious than . . . (others) . . . as it
enables the monopolists to plead that they are acting in the
interests of those whom they are in fact excluding. They can
claim that they are raising the standard of living of the very
ones whose competition they wish to eliminate, and even get
the support of legal enactment to enable them to carry out
their policy."[25]

In this way we have returned to our starting point, and we
can now assert again, not in the company of "orthodox" economists (as those whose arguments cannot be refuted are called
in order to discredit them), but together with a group that cannot be suspect since it is made up of Keynes, Lloyd George,
Muir, Simon, and some other politicians and economists, that
"the improved wages have not been primarily or even mainly
due to the work of the Trade Unions. They could have
achieved very little if the wealth of the nation had not been
increasing; and the primary cause of the rise of wages has been
an increase of efficiency in the production of wealth."[26] We
shall also be forced to acknowledge that the best wage rates are
not the highest ones, but those that result in full employment
and a maximum total income of the working class as a whole,
and this not from the point of view of capitalists or entrepreneurs, but in terms of what is more interesting and worthy of
attention, the well-being of the workers.

Wages Under Socialism

Before proceeding to other topics and leaving this subject of
wages which has engaged our attention so long and justifiably
so, I wish to deal with a problem whose omission would give
ground for arguing that this discussion is incomplete, and con-

---

[25]Hutt, *op. cit.*, p. 19.
[26]Quoted in *The American Individual Enterprise System*, v.I. pp. 159–160.

sequently for rejecting my conclusions. It has been shown that workers are not the victims of exploitation since they receive the full product of their labor save in the abnormal case of monopoly. I believe I have proved that an artificial, forced rise in wages not only does not benefit the laboring masses, but harms them and sets them back. However, there is a final aspect to be considered. It is possible that everything I have written will be admitted, but that the rejoinder may be made immediately that my analysis is valid only on the assumptions that I started from, i.e., within a market economy or a regime of free enterprise. But if we reject this system of economic organization, the basis for valuing labor will no longer be the price determined by its marginal productivity, we shall throw off the shackles of the normal wage rate and of the other concepts that I have used, and we shall at last be able to compensate labor according to worthier standards than the supply of workers, the whims of consumers, and the resultant demand for personal services. We shall be in a position to establish a system of real social justice, in which wages will not be those set by the market, but fair wages that will satisfy our feeling of what is just and right.

I am going to deal with the appealing but confused theory to which I refer, because I consider that my work will not be as useful as I would wish if I leave some loose ends, and do not face up to all the ideas that have been brought forward in relation to the so-called labor question. Although I sympathize sincerely with the impulses that animate the authors of this criticism, I have to state that the criticism starts from a fundamental error regarding the nature of economic science, that it is wrong in mixing situations which it should examine separately. This opinion represents a futile attempt to escape from the conclusions that derive from the analysis that I have carried out, and that it is open to other critical observations which it has been unable to counter so far. But let us proceed gradually to introduce order into the discussion and to cast light on this matter, since the first defect I find in this opinion consists in its confusion.

No one denies that social institutions may undergo profound changes and that, specifically, the economic organization to which the adjectives "capitalist" or "liberal" are applied (and which is described as a market society or a free-enterprise system) may be superseded by some other. But from this undoubted fact, it does not follow that the science which has been slowly built up to study economic phenomena is not relevant to all their manifestations and, therefore, to those that may occur in a collectivistic community, for example. It is also true that up to now, for historical reasons as well as for the sake of expediency, economics has devoted itself almost exclusively to the study of such phenomena as the market, prices, exchange, economic calculation, etc. However, one would have to be one hundred years behind the times intellectually to hold that economics is the science of only one part of our lives, that is, the "economic" side of human conduct or the science of wealth and egotism. Ever since what Robbins calls the "Mengerian Revolution"[27] (incidentally, this was a real revolution), economics has stood for a great deal more than that. The modern theory of value laid the foundations for transforming economics into a general science of human action. Consequently, neither a socialist community nor the unstable state of affairs which is designated under the name of interventionism, can escape from its scrutiny and conclusions. If this were not so, one would be at a loss to understand why the problem of economic calculation constitutes the crucial difficulty of socialism and why no less a personage than the communist, Professor Lange, has proposed that Professor Mises (who was the first to demonstrate that it is impossible in a socialist community, although Lange is of the opinion that the problem can be solved), should have a statue in the marble halls of the Central Planning Council of the social organization of the future.[28]

As mistaken as the statement that it is feasible to do with-

[27]Robbins, *op. cit.*, p. 106.
[28]According to reference by Hayek in *Individualism and Economic Order*, The University of Chicago Press, 1948, p. 89.

out economics, is the belief that labor can be valued according to other principles than the ones declared by this disagreeable discipline, which prevents us from ascending to the azure heights of fantasy. Let us assume that there are no prices, as there cannot be in a socialist system. Then, labor will not be remunerated by means of a wage that will tend to correspond to its marginal productivity but according to other criteria. From this it does not follow that we can do without the theory of the marginal productivity of labor. The latter is not an explanation of the process by which prices are formed, but a theory of value. Therefore, even if some other pricing and distributing procedure is adopted, different from that of a free market, labor will not be worth more as a result. If it is abundant, and if the other factors of production are scarce, its yield will necessarily continue to be low. If this were not true, we should expect China to become at any moment the richest nation in the world, since communism prevails there and since it will be possible to forget everything that economics teaches.

Aside from other insurmountable obstacles to an improvement in the condition of the workers in a socialist regime (in particular the one mentioned; namely, that it will be definitely inferior to the capitalist system because it will lack the help of economic calculation, so that production will be carried on blindly) even in this sort of society, the primary requirement for working people to receive more consists in an increase in the total product.

Wages Under Interventionism

In an economic system in which neither private property nor the market nor freedom of occupation nor the free choice of consumers is suppressed, and in which it is only their operation that is modified (or more precisely, in which it is the results of their free operation that an attempt is made to alter, in order that they may coincide with the ethical ideals of the people in favor of the alteration) there is no reason why my arguments and conclusions should not be applicable. As is

well known, that economic system is interventionism, which
is given this name because the characteristic means for seeking
to attain its end consist in an act of intervention by the government, usually an order or a prohibition. But the truth is
that interventionism does not represent a third way or solution, nor a genuine economic system different from socialism
and capitalism, but this same system, supposedly reformed
and improved, and with its alleged unfavorable features and
abuses eliminated.

Since the starting point of the whole discussion is the con-
tention that the wage rates as determined by the market are
too low, we can expect that in the immense majority of instances just wages would be higher. It is evident that the employers will not make up the difference voluntarily because
the market does not force them to do so, and that the government or the labor unions will have to do it in their place. The
means that they will resort to for this purpose will be the same
ones that we have studied, backed up in the last resort, by
coercion and the power of the state. Consequently, this long
analysis is nothing but a study of the effects of just wages on
the economic process and on the well-being and advancement
of workers. The only new feature is the term "just wage,"
instead of which I spoke of artificially raised wages or of wages
higher than those that would be normal in a free market, in
order to permit an objective consideration of the questions
involved and to eliminate the sentimental and other connota-
tions that an expression such as "a just wage" inevitably im-
plies.

But we should not limit ourselves to the field that we have
surveyed. Let us go beyond it and explore other possibilities.
It may be that forcing the employer to make up the difference
that is necessary in order to round out a fair wage for the
worker is not justified, besides being harmful. This measure is
due to social reasons, and its objectives are also social. Consequently, the correct solution is for the state to pay this part,
this supplement to wages.

This solution cannot be taken seriously. The state is not

something apart from the community, but the community itself, regarded from a special point of view; namely, from the standpoint of certain functions for whose performance the only monopoly that is permissible in a free society is created, the monopoly of coercion and force. Much less can the state be conceived as an entity standing outside of the social process of production or above it, and possessing resources of its own, with which to make gifts to us, like a Santa Claus for adults. The truth is that this proposal is equivalent to asking us to vote ourselves a subsidy which will come out of our own pockets. Once again, the fundamental obstacle which prevents Mexican workers from enjoying the ample wages that American working men receive is not the fact that a capitalistic system exists by and large on this side of the Rio Grande, or that our entrepreneurs display greater covetousness or avarice, it consists simply in the fact that our production per head is many times lower than that of our neighbors, because the latter do not work alone, but aided by the greatest accumulation of capital in history. Therefore, one should not wonder that the total to be distributed, as well as the share that goes to each one, is very small in Mexico. As a result, the amount that the government would be able to distribute, after taking it away from some of us by means of new taxes, would be minute and would not alter the present situation in a significant way. Its real effect would be to decrease the total amount to be distributed, as well as producing other serious evils which it seems unnecessary to point out.

Wages and "Justice"

Fundamentally the same answer must be given to another solution which is sure to be advanced, but which is worthy of more careful consideration. Why should it be necessary for the government to mediate in order to settle matters between workers and employers, it may be asked. Why should not businessmen themselves pay those who collaborate with them the compensation to which justice entitles them? For this it will suffice that they be guided by the teachings of morality and righteousness instead of being impelled by the profit motive and egotism. In this way it will be possible to satisfy the requirements of social justice, and there will be no question of asking for help from that other present-day monster, the dreadful and all-absorbing state.

Just as in the preceding case, if wages are insufficient for a worker to lead the suitable and ample life that we wish for him, one should not search for the basic causes of this situation in the imperfection of social institutions or even in that of human nature. One should seek them in the scarcity which constitutes the original and primary fact with which nature faces us and in the relation between the element of labor and the other factors of production. "The first problem of reform in any system of distribution," writes an economist, "is to search for the limiting factor or factors . . . The remedy is, of course, to increase the supply of the limiting factors . . . It is a common error to suppose that justice would eliminate poverty . . . If each one gets only what he produces, or what he is worth, and if he does not produce enough to live upon, or if he is not worth enough as a worker to earn a wage which will support him, he will still be poor. Before we can eliminate poverty, therefore, . . . we must also see to it that each one is made worth enough or productive enough to enable him to live comfortably upon his earnings."[29]

I shall not be content to triumph so easily over this solution which is notoriously worthy of respect because of the ground on which it conducts the discussion and of its moderate and prudent tendencies. According to it, the self-interest which constitutes the motive force behind each participant in the process of production (not only entrepreneurs but the owners of natural resources and of capital, and workers in no lesser degree) should be replaced by the virtues of fairness, righteousness, altruism, and charity. Let us forget the undeniable

[29]Carver, Thomas Nixon, *Essays in Social Justice*, Harvard University Press, Cambridge, 1940, pp. 358 and 359.

41

fact that men have not shown themselves tractable to these exhortations, and that a transformation such as we have not seen until now would be necessary before the new behavior that is recommended could be accepted in earnest. The truth is that the very concepts that are proposed, of fair prices and fair wages, are fallacious and incapable of providing a dependable guide for economic transactions. The moment one passes from generalities to particulars, or from the abstract field in which these dissertations take place, to the concrete one of the problems presented by the realities of the market, rectitude, as well as the other qualities mentioned, turns out to be incapable of solving them. With all the good faith in the world, the two parties to an economic relation will maintain different points of view, just as they do now. However high it may be, no wage seems unfair to a working man. Similarly, no profit will be considered as excessive by an entrepreneur. It is only the general and impersonal discipline of the market that makes it possible to adjust their dissimilar opinions at present. If we do not have the market, where shall we turn for a decision on what is a fair wage in each case and for a solution to the interminable controversies that will surely arise?

The answer is predictable. In the first place, it will be said that the parties themselves cannot give a fair decision because they stand to gain or lose in the conflict and are liable to err, so that we must turn to other, more competent and impartial persons. Although this really amounts to confessing that the solution cannot work because the starting point was that it was up to those concerned to make it operate successfully, let us assume that the workers and the employer agree to go before the wisest and most virtuous of men. Let us suppose that he earnestly strives to reach a solution that will satisfy our sentiment of justice and which will conform to all other virtues mentioned before, instead of proceeding as labor arbitrators do, who only look for a way out between the fifteen dollars increase demanded by the workers and the five dollars offered by the employer. What criteria will he consider to determine a just wage? According to the unpleasantness of the work and the effort it demands? It is justifiable to state that there does not exist any objective means of estimating the disutility of labor. Will he take into account the worker's needs? To determine the worker's need raises such grave difficulties, moral, practical and of every sort, that even the socialist regimes have been forced to abandon the lovely formula "to each according to his needs," in order to look for more feasible ways of effective distribution. Will he be guided by the financial capacity of the firm? It can be shown that this system would be ruinous for a country and is indefensible ethically and even practically. So I return to the question: What really and truthfully constitutes a fair wage?

It is as impossible to find an answer to this question as it is to give concrete meaning to the concept of a just price, which philosophers and theologians have sought in vain to do for centuries. Hayek has shown that there is no comprehensive scale of values, no complete moral code, that would permit an authoritative decision to the problems that our present society leaves to be settled by the free interaction of individuals.[30] Knight's position regarding the question that interests us is even more radical because he holds that "when both wages and justice are clearly and correctly defined, the expression combining the two words is largely self-contradictory or redundant." The result is that "just or unjust wages has little or more meaning than a just or unjust turn of the weather at some particular juncture of human affairs."[31] Far from my thesis having been refuted, one must complement it by saying that the only justice which is attainable in this world, both regarding wages and the shares that go to the other agents of production, consists in having each one of them obtain the remuneration which corresponds to the productivity of its contribution to the economic process.

[30]Hayek, F., in *The Road to Serfdom,* University of Chicago Press, Chicago, 1944, pp. 56f.
[31]Knight, *op. cit.,* p. 5.

The Economics of Non-Wage Elements in Labor Costs

There are still several important points to be dealt with. I shall not go into the measures which result in safer, healthier, or more comfortable working conditions, because the introduction of these improvements or other steps conducive to the same end increase costs as a general rule, and their economic effect is essentially similar to that of a rise in wages. I will not discuss the problems relating to the worker's economic security, because they are evidently connected with questions of a general character that go far beyond my stated purpose. It is of interest that the costs of the benefits paid in addition to wages devolve upon the workers, even if it is the employer who is bound by law or through custom to disburse them. Economic analysis points out that the notion that these supplements are so many gifts for the wage-earner is erroneous, in spite of the common habit of calling them "social advances" or "conquests of the workers," because in the final instance they reduce the net wages. In the specific case of social insurance, the cost of contributions falls finally upon the workers, whatever the legal provisions on the subject. Although the employer will pay more for the labor factor at the outset, immediately thereafter all the consequences which I indicated in studying wages will take place. In the long run, the only result will be partial or institutional unemployment.

The reduction in working hours, the limitation of night work, and the prohibition of some kinds of work to women and to children below a certain age present both resemblances to and differences from the problem of wages which have been discussed previously. The difference consists in the fact that this variety of interventionism (I use this expression because my remarks are applicable only when we assume that changes are established by means of official coercion or through the pressure exerted by labor unions, and not when they are a result of the operation of a free market) does not represent an interference with the data of the market, but is an example of restrictionism, that is, of acts which make production more difficult and tend to reduce it. It cannot be argued, as public opinion holds, that these kinds of measures constitute one more victory for the workers, which can by no means harm them and whose burden will fall wholly on the employer. Since their effect is to diminish the available labor force, we must indeed admit that they raise the marginal productivity of labor while lowering that of capital. But inasmuch as they simultaneously diminish the total volume of goods that is produced, their necessary consequence must be a general impoverishment. The proportional share alloted to the workers in the distribution of social income will be larger, but it will be computed with relation to a smaller total amount. Whether their income really increases or decreases will depend on the concrete facts of a given state of affairs.

I have previously assumed that the reduction in the working day does not affect the cost of labor. If we suppose instead, in spite of the reduction, that the daily or weekly wages do not vary, that is, that at the same time the reduction goes into effect, the employer is forced to continue to pay the same wages, obviously, his outlay for the item of personal services will not change, but the yield, the result he obtained in return, will decrease. As the amount produced decreases, so the sales, the income, and consequently the profits of the firm will lessen. On this hypothesis, which we must expect to be one that will occur most frequently in practice, in view of the power that labor unions have achieved and of the widespread belief that the employer is the only one harmed by "prolabor" policies, the same phenomena of withdrawal and noninvestment of capital, as well as of shrinking of employment opportunities, that we observed in the case of wage rates above those set by the market, will come into play.

However, one point should be clarified. There must be an exception of the optimum working day. The measures being analyzed, besides providing the workers with greater leisure, which is one of the ends that all of us pursue as a result of the primary and unavoidable fact of the disutility of labor, may result in other important advantages from the point of view of general health, social peace, and opportunities for self-improvement. It must be emphasized that from an economic point of view, these advantages represent a cost instead of an item of income and that such a cost falls upon the whole community (of which the workers form the most numerous group) and not upon capital, which is essentially mobile in the short run, nor upon entrepreneurs, whose profits or losses are not affected by "prolabor" policies, since they depend upon their greater or smaller success in adjusting to the changing conditions of the market.

If the "prolabor" policy limited itself to inflicting on the workers and, more generally, on a nation's economy, the mischiefs which I have explained, we could deplore such occurrences and hope that these interventionist measures will not assume such proportions as to nullify the forces that are incessantly at work in an otherwise free economy and that lead it toward progress and well-being. In the special case of Mexico, a country that offers attractions and advantages from an economic viewpoint, there is no doubt that the harmful effects of labor legislation, as long as this does not go beyond certain limits, will be offset by the other factors making for our general development, which will be thereby retarded, as it has indeed been up to now, but not obstructed completely. My present purpose is to call attention to other evils which the prevailing tendency brings in its train. Although they are less specific than the ones described heretofore, they have become so widespread and have assumed such an alarming and even ominous character everywhere in the world, that they should evoke the deepest and most conscientious meditation on the part of all those who desire to preserve our civilization and our way of life.

Marxist Objections

The Marxist doctrine of a class struggle has been refuted so many times and from such a diversity of points of view that there are few who will defend it on the intellectual plane in this day and age. Presumably, no one will dare to espouse it on moral grounds, especially in view of the fact that even Marxists do not regard it as good in itself, but exclusively as an instrument for destroying the capitalist society. We must grant them that they are right in this, since in the variegated and deceitful bag of tricks employed by communism, none has shown more confusion nor become more effective than its preachment that the factors of production are divided by insoluble conflicts. Unfortunately, except for free-market thinkers, there has not been the clear-cut denial and the determined attitude of opposition which such a radically false and dangerous doctrine should arouse. The other schools of thought, although they deplore class struggles, seem to accept the Marxist assertions more than half-way, and many of them subscribe to the basic thesis that the system of private ownership of the means of production benefits the small group of capitalists and entrepreneurs, and injures the rights and interests of a majority of the population. This position is even more exaggerated and visible in the labor movement, as a result of the failure to understand the workings of the market and of the untenable thesis of labor exploitation which we have found at the basis of the espousal of the measures I have criticized.

There can be no doubt, in view of the foregoing analysis, that the acceptance of the intellectual and ethical foundation of so-called labor claims (I am not referring to their acceptance in practice, because they may be justified in concrete instances, either for political reasons or for the sake of expediency) contributes very powerfully toward extending the principles of the doctrine of the class struggle and toward strengthening the conviction that they are true and that such a struggle is morally right. At the same time, this ideology makes workers discontented and neurotic, ready to create greater difficulties and even to support revolutionary movements. The worker refuses to accept the effort that all labor demands and the unpleasantness that it entails, as facts that we cannot shirk (at least since our fathers were expelled from

47

the Garden of Eden) and becomes a victim of socialist propaganda. Such propaganda, in common with all Utopias, prom-
ises him that the disutility of labor will fade away and that
it will change into a pleasure and a source of delight. In this
way the confusion that lies at the basis of the so-called labor
question becomes worse, and the soil is prepared for class
struggles and for the further objectives for which this doctrine
has proved itself such an efficient instrument.

Prolabor Policy and Market Distortions

Wage rates above the market level, as well as the other
measures of the "prolabor" policy now in vogue, represent an
effort to alter the working of the market in a certain direction.
It should not surprise us, therefore, that their general and
mediate effects on the market and on a free economy (of
which the market constitutes the central and most important
organ) should also be acutely unfavorable and even upsetting.
"The structure of wages produced by collective bargaining
is unfavorable to the achievement of the largest national output for two reasons. One reason is that it prevents industry
from producing goods in the most advantageous proportions.
The other reason is that it produces 'wage-distortion unemployment' and thus limits the output of industry."[32] Although
they differ in the arguments that they advance, many other
economists concur in this opinion. Thus, and referring especially to the raising of wages in backward areas (such as the
South in the United States) so as to equal those in the North
and East and to prevent them from competing with the wages
paid by factories located in those latter parts of the country,
Simons points out that such a forced increase will make it
more difficult for the southern States to industrialize and to
progress.[33] Other writers call attention to the fact that like all

[32]Hutt, *op. cit.*, p. 73.
[33]Simons, *op. cit.*, pp. 134–138.

monopolies, those that occur in the field of labor are opposed to change and that their watchword is stability. In other words, they resist stubbornly all adjustments and particularly any modification of wages except in an upward direction. In this way the economy becomes rigid and unadaptable, in spite of the fact that the only way of co-ordinating production to the highly variable conditions that result from the perpetually fluctuating desires and opinions of consumers, from scientific and technological progress, from the phenomena of nature, and from a hundred more circumstances, consists in not hampering the movements of the market. "The flexibility of commodity prices and wage rates," concludes Mises, "is the vehicle of adjustment, improvement, and progress. Those who condemn changes in prices and wages as unjust and who ask for the preservation of what they call just, are in fact combating endeavors to make economic conditions more satisfactory."[34]

Prolabor Policy and Inflation

Among the most notorious consequences of the mischiefs described are the monetary effects, or more precisely, the inflationary effects, of the supposedly prolabor policy. Wolman limits himself to expressing a fact that can be observed throughout the world when he states that "national unions become, next to the government, the most effective cost-and-price-raising instruments of modern times."[35] As we already saw, the corollary to the reduction of sales and profits that follows on an artificial rise in wages is the need to decrease the number of workers employed. When dealing with factors that may hide from view, for a longer or shorter time, the harm done by these measures, it was noted that inflation or credit

[34]Mises, *op. cit.*, p. 723.

[35]Wolman, Leo, *Industry-Wide Bargaining*, The Foundation for Economic Education, Irvington-on-Hudson, 1948, p. 52.

expansion may prevent or delay the appearance of unemployment. These phenomena should be analyzed more closely and their general effects on the economy noted.

There are two ways for a government to prevent unemployment. First, it can approve a program to expand its activities and finance it through inflation. If new taxes are levied and collected for the purpose of obtaining the funds needed to meet the increased expenditures required by such a plan, taxpayers will have correspondingly less money for their needs. They will have to economize on their spending, and what will be gained in jobs created by public authorities will be lost in those sectors which the effects of the official program will not reach. If the government turns to inflationary procedures, we shall not have this difficulty: consumers will have the same tax burden as before, they will not have to skimp on their spending, and the newly created jobs will represent a net gain as regards the total of employment opportunities. But this is only the first step in what will in time turn into a giddy race. With more money in circulation, prices will tend to rise. The margin of profit to entrepreneurs, which had shrunk as a result of the increase in wages, will stretch out again. Consequently, there will be no reason for unemployment to spread. Some industries that had closed down will resume operations, and more workers will be hired. With this, the first phase of the inflation comes to an end, a phase that is purely recuperative, and we enter the second stage.

Once the prices of goods and services go up, buyers will be seriously harmed. Whether they realize what is the initial cause of the rise in living costs, or whether they begin to clamor against speculators and profiteers, as is usually the case, it is probable that they will try to increase their income and ask for a raise in wages. Compensation for services will go up, in some cases voluntarily, in others, after strikes or the intervention of labor authorities. Once this takes place, the same process previously described, of increased costs, lessened sales and profits, reduced operations, and unemployment, will start again. The only way to prevent it will be to inject new quantities of money, which will have to be progressively larger. Moreover, since, in view of the higher level of prices and wages, the sums that were put into circulation formerly will no longer be sufficient.

It is important to describe in detail the process whereby inflations get under way, notwithstanding the fact that they have become all too frequent and familiar, so that we may perceive clearly how they eliminate the conditions created by artificially raised wages. At the same time, attention should be called to the problem we face in the present-day world. In a recent cartoon, a man wearing the word "wage" is running after his shadow, which bears the label "cost of living." Needless to say, he does not catch up with it. But the dangerous part of this is that the race takes place in the direction of an abyss, which also is given a name, "inflation."

We can read news about this race everyday in the newspapers in the United States, South America and Mexico where it is only fair to admit that the problem has not reached the acute stage that it has in Argentina, Bolivia, Brazil or Chile. However, there can be no doubt that inflation deepens economic differences between the two classes that have been in the process of formation. At the same time, the hardships and poverty of the class composed of nonunionized workers who are the overwhelming majority of our population, are intensified.

Simultaneously and as a result of the constant rise in their costs, our industries, already in need of customs protection, become more incapable of meeting foreign competition. Protective duties are no longer sufficient to offset the advantages enjoyed by foreign industries, so that they undergo a change and become a concealed means for the government to force consumers to subsidize the workers' gains. But these aspects should not worry us most. The truth is that our industries have reached the point of pricing themselves out of the domestic market. A well-known newspaperman was asking himself a few days ago how it is possible that when there are 8 or 10 million people in our country who do not wear shoes, if we at the same time have factories which are capable of providing them, they do not produce shoes at their full capacity. The answer is very simple: because shoeless people do not have the necessary economic capacity for buying footwear. But a further cause that contributes to this situation is to be found in the progressively rising and alarming costs of industrial production which has resulted in setting the prices of most products far beyond the reach of the great mass of our population.

Labor Unions as Monopolies

I have several times referred to monopolistic labor unions and practices. The meaning of this charge should be clarified. To begin with, it is a commonplace observation among students of labor relations that unions have achieved monopoly positions and that they act as such every day. It is at least indisputable that their practices restrict competition even if, as some authors contend, they do not fulfill all the characteristics of a monopoly. Their favorite means of action is to prevent other workers from entering those lines of occupation which they exploit. This is accomplished by imposing higher wage rates than those determined by the situation of the market, as well as through a diversity of entrance requirements designed to make sure of a reserved enclosure and to place themselves beyond the reach of competition. "When the public undertook to encourage unions," Slichter states, "it thought that it was helping downtrodden and oppressed men to help themselves. It did not foresee the great power that it was placing in the hands of a few men."[36] In another work, characterized by its sympathetic attitude toward labor unions, nevertheless there is an observation that "while in the beginning unions were organized to protect the workers against intolerable abuses, as they have gained power, they have often

[36]Slichter, *op. cit.*, p. 25.

become in themselves abusive, so that society now sometimes needs protection against them."[37]

As regards the degree of power attained by these organizations, for instance in the United States, it is worth while pondering that "the strongest unions . . . are the most powerful economic organizations which the country has ever seen. One cannot conceive of the railroads, even if they were not bound by law to render continuous service, daring to cut off the country from railroad service. Steel producers would not dare combine for the purpose of depriving the country of steel. No combination of coal operators would dare cut off the supply of coal. Yet in each of these industries during the last year (1946) unions have not hesitated to stop production to enforce their demands, in some cases, very trivial demands."[38] In these times, when such a dangerous situation prevails so much like war that the only thing lacking is to call it by this name, the railroadmen's unions do not hesitate to call a strike, and the President of the most powerful nation on earth is reduced to begging them to behave and to addressing them with friendly remonstrances. Should anyone be surprised if, in view of incidents of this kind, other countries become emboldened and feel encouraged to set forth on the road to aggression and conquest?

"In an economy of intricate division of labor, every large organized group is in a position at any time to disrupt or to stop the whole flow of social income." This statement, which before the rise of labor unionism would have given the world a rude shock and sounded a call of alarm, is nothing more than the bald statement of a fact to which we are becoming more accustomed with every day that goes by. But let us listen to the inference that the eminent author of "Economic Policy for a Free Society" draws from it. "The system must soon break down if groups persist in exercising that power or

[37]Bye, Raymond T. and Hewett, William W., *Applied Economics*, Appleton, Century, Crofts, Inc., New York and London, 1947, p. 170.
[38]Slichter, *op. cit.*, pp. 14–15.

if they must continuously be bribed to forego its disastrous exercise."[39]

It will not be difficult to explain such an alarming conclusion. A free economy cannot endure without the institution of the market. A free market does not exist except in name if prices are not formed freely. Indeed, free economy, free market, and free prices are but different names for the same thing. The acknowledged objective of the leaders of the labor movement is to do away with wages as prices and with the labor market. This is the case even when their aim is not frankly revolutionary, as it is with Laski and those socialists or communists who have infiltrated the unions, and when they do not regard labor agitation as a step toward the regimented world of their dreams. Wages do not appear except in certain forms of production or in a special economic sector. They are present in every productive process, together with the three other agents isolated by analysis. Among them, the labor factor is invested with chief importance because, as mentioned before, it represents the largest element in regard to cost and because it receives up to four-fifths of the national income. If this agent of production is withdrawn from competition, and if it is no longer subject to the principles of a free economy, the fatal result will be the bankruptcy and disappearance of this form of organization.

After the foregoing reasoning, which appears to be irrefutable, further insistence on this point would seem superfluous. Government interference in labor relations (that proceeding from labor unions has the same character, whether by its toleration or by delegation), like other varieties of interventionism, does not constitute a complete system. It is not stable, and does not represent a permanent form of economic organization. Instead, it is a partial and unstable system, and represents a form that is essentially transitory. Consequently, either we abstain from it and return to a free economy, or we

[39]Simons, *op. cit.*, p. 122.

go on regulating and interfering until we reach complete control and a totalitarian economy.

Lindblom states that "an increasing number of economists believe that union pressure on wages is a, perhaps *the*, major economic problem of our time" . . . and "that unionism and the private enterprise economy are incompatible; that once unions become strong, the attempt to maintain our economy as it now stands produces unemployment or inflation."[40] This long recital of the general evils that accompany a "prolabor" policy, which at first sight has limited objectives that seem plausible and innocent, can be concluded with another statement from Lindblom: "The gigantic work stoppages which have occurred since the war have diverted everyone's attention from the long-run consequences of unionism. The strike is a crucially important immediate problem which we cannot ignore. It paralyses production, and it is dramatic. But the real labor problem is its aftermath. To believe otherwise is to mistake peace for order and the beginning for the end. For if wage disputes call a halt to production temporarily, their settlement may disorganize it permanently. Unionism will destroy the price system by what it wins rather than by the struggle to win it. It sabotages the competitive order, not because the economy cannot weather the disturbance of work stoppages but because it cannot produce high output and employment at union wage rates. Nor can the economy survive the union's systematic disorganization of markets and its persistent undercutting of managerial authority."[41]

Summary

It may now be worthwhile to recall briefly our starting point. The problem consisted in finding out whether the almost uni-

---

[40]Lindblom, *Unions and Capitalism*, Yale University Press, New Haven, 1949, p. V.

[41]Lindblom, *op. cit.*, p. 5.

versal belief that the improvement in the condition of the workers is due to the governments and the labor unions, is correct. Although presenting a negative reply from a variety of viewpoints, and showing that attempts to escape from it are doomed to failure, I assert once again that, besides being most tenacious and dangerous, this belief is wholly false. It is not labor legislation or union pressure that has raised wages, shortened the hours of toil, and made it possible for women and children to leave the factories. If wages have risen, if workers have more free time, and if the labor of women and children is no longer necessary, it is because of the increase in productivity per man hour. In turn, this higher productivity has been a result of scientific and technological advances, which have been applied and made use of, thanks to the enormous investments that the accumulation of capital has made possible. The reasoning that, seeing economic progress as a concomitant of labor legislation and the prevalence of unions, concludes that the former has been produced by the latter, is simplistic and defective. It is as unfounded as the belief by the rooster in the fable that it was its crowing that caused the sun to rise.

Some people will not fail to bring up the trite case of the conditions that followed upon the Industrial Revolution and to contend that it was due to the Factory Acts and subsequent regulations that the conditions were eliminated. This is not the time to undertake a study of the interpretation of that great economic and social phenomenon, which has been dealt with by many authors, especially historians of the labor movement. Practically without exception, says Hutt, these historians have been openly hostile to orthodox theory.[42] Neither is it possible to go into the popular defamation suffered by the Industrial Revolution, particularly at the hands of some writers on labor law. Suffice it to repeat with a well-documented work, that "a better knowledge of the period anterior to 1760 is teaching us that unemployment, low wages and child labor

---

[42]Hutt, *op. cit.*, p. 11.

were no new phenomena at that date."[43] Or to conclude as does another balanced and complete summary that "Of labor conditions no easy generalization is possible. Long hours, child labor, employment of women, insanitary conditions, payment in truck, unemployment, low wages, capitalistic tyranny, labor unrest, industrial fatigue, occupational diseases and the 'cash nexus' were not inventions of industrial factory capitalism . . . the industrial revolution increased rather than decreased the material welfare of the mass of the population . . . Unfortunately much of our view of the social aspects of the revolution is drawn from reports of official investigations which in their very nature are full of complaints and grievances."[44] The truth is that, however unfavorable prevailing conditions may have been, in the existing circumstances they represented the best possible alternatives, as is proved by the fact that the workers chose them. We can deplore the fact that such a state of affairs should have existed, but it is a mistake to blame these conditions on the new industries or on the entrepreneurs. One must seek for their causes in the economic organization of the precapitalist era, in the grinding scarcity of capital, in technological and commercial backwardness, in the coarseness of public and private mores, in the wars and upheavals of the times, and in other factors.

Far from having been responsible for the poverty of the masses, the new system of production was nothing less than the means of raising them to a condition which had never before been imagined, of multiplying their numbers also in an unprecedented way, and of creating the prosperity and comfort to which we have become accustomed that we regard them as something given and natural. We forget that the primary state of mankind, which it had no hope of bettering until a period that represents an insignificant fraction of its history, was hunger, privation, and impotence. The progress

[43]Buer, M. C., *Health, Wealth and Population in the Early Days of the Industrial Revolution*, Routledge, London, 1926, pp. 58 and 59.
[44]Herbert Heaton, in article "Industrial Revolution," in the *Encyclopedia of the Social Sciences*, The Macmillan Company, New York, 1935, v.8, p. 12.

that was achieved was not the inevitable result of a natural law. It was due to the fact that circumstances were favorable, that the obstacles which until then had hindered or stifled individual initiative, the formation of capital, scientific discoveries, and the introduction of new methods in technology and organization were removed.

Today the constellation of elements is unpropitious, and as the result of a great paradox, of one of those tragic anomalies with which history presents us, the improvement achieved in the condition of workingmen and the incomparable progress in all respects to which I refer, coincide with the repudiation of everything that made them possible. They coincide with a revolutionary and destructionist propaganda based on a profound ignorance and on the most violent and absurd charges against the existing social order. In the institutional complex created by these ideas, labor legislation, labor unions, and the various means of action studied, represent so many components which are not only not conducive to the end on which all of us agree, of plenty and well-being, but which are definitely opposed to the operation and even to the subsistence of the only system of production that has been able to turn those goals into realities.

For poor nations like Mexico, which are lacking in capital, and where we have countless masses deprived of everything indispensable to life, this problem is decisive. If we allow ourselves to be deluded by spurious doctrines of pseudo-laborism, we shall extinguish the splendid impulse that has been activated in these last years. We shall condemn several millions of our brothers to destitution and starvation, for whom our country's industrialization and economic development would mean the only real and well-founded hope of salvation.

Bibliography

Academy of Political Science, *Labor Policy and Labor Relations.* Columbia University, New York, May, 1946.

Academy of Political Science, *Prices, Wages and Inflation.* Columbia University, New York, May, 1948.

Azpiazu, Joaquin, *Las Directrices Sociales de la Iglesia Católica. (Guidelines of the Catholic Church.)* Spanish Bibliographic Editors, Madrid, 1950.

Backman, Jules, *Wages and Prices.* The Foundation for Economic Education, Inc., Irvington-on-Hudson, New York, 1947.

Bakke, E. Wight, John F. Dunlop, Fritz Machlup, Felix Morley, Jacob Viner and Leo Wolman, *Wage Determination and the Economics of Liberalism.* Chamber of Commerce of the United States, Washington, 1947.

Benham, Frederic, *Curso Superior de Económica.* Fondo de Cultura Económica, Mexico, 1941. *Economics.* Isaac Pitman and Sons, London, 1948.

Bradley, Philip D., (Editor), *The Public Stake in Union Power.* The University of Virginia Press, Charlottesville, 1959.

Briefs, Goetz, *Unionism Reappraised, From Classical Unionism to Union Establishment.* American Enterprise Association, Washington, 1960.

Brozen, Yale, "The Effect of Statutory Minimum Wage Increases on Teen-Age Unemployment." *The Journal of Law and Economics,* XII (1). The University of Chicago Law School, Chicago, April, 1969.

Brozen, Yale and Milton Friedman, *The Minimum Wage Rate—Who Really Pays?* The Free Society Association, Washington, 1966.

Bye, Raymond T., *Principles of Economics.* F. A. Crofts & Co., New York, 1947.

Bye, Raymond T. and William W. Hewett, *Applied Economics.* Appleton-Century-Crofts, Inc., New York and London, 1947.

Cannan, Edwin, *Repaso a la Teoria Económica.* Fondo de Cultura Económica, Mexico, 1940. *Review of Economic Theory.* P. S. King and Son, London, 1929.

Carver, Thomas Nixon, *Essays in Social Justice.* Harvard University Press, Cambridge, 1940.

Chamber of Commerce of the United States, *Wage Determination and the Economics of Liberalism.* Washington, 1947.

Chamberlin, Edward H., Philip D. Bradley, Gerald D. Reilly and Roscoe Pound, *Labor Unions and Public Policy.* American Enterprise Association, Washington, 1958.

Clark, John Bates, *The Distribution of Wealth.* Macmillan, New York, 1902.

Confederacion Patronal de la Republica Mexicana, *El Contrato Colectivo de Trabajo.* (Employers Federation of Mexico, *Collective Labor Agreements.*) Mexico, 1949.

Confederacion Patronal de la Republica Mexicana, *Modernizacion de las Relaciones de Trabajo.* (*Modernization of Labor Relations.*) Mexico, 1949.

Cox, Jacob D., *The Economic Basis of Fair Wages.* The Ronald Press Company, New York, 1926.

De la Cueva, Mario, *Derecho Mexicana del Trabajo.* (*Mexican Labor Law.*) Librer de Porrua Hnos. y Cia., Mexico, 1943 y 1949.

Dobb, Maurice, *Salarios.* Fondo de Cultura Economica. Mexico, 1941. *Wages.* Cambridge University Press, 1946.

Dunlop, John T., *The Theory of Wage Determination.* Macmillan, New York, 1957.

Dunlop, John T., *Wage Determination under Trade Unions.* Macmillan, New York, 1944.

Ellis, Howard S. (Editor), *A Survey of Contemporary Economics.* The American Economic Association, Philadelphia, Toronto, 1948.

Fairchild, Fred Rogers, *Profits and the Ability to Pay Wages.* The

Foundation for Economic Education, Inc., Irvington-on-Hudson, New York, 1946.

Hagenbuch, Walter, *Social Economics*. Cambridge University Press, 1958.

Harper, F. A., *The Crisis of the Free Market*. National Industrial Conference Board, Inc., New York, 1945.

Harper, F. A., *Why Wages Rise*. The Foundation for Economic Education, Irvington-on-Hudson, New York, 1957.

Hazlitt, Henry, *Economics in One Lesson*. Harper & Brothers, New York and London, 1946.

Hicks, J. R., *The Theory of Wages*. Peter Smith, New York, 1948.

Hutt, W. H., *The Economics of the Colour Bar*. The Institute of Economic Affairs, London, 1964.

Hutt, W. H., *The Theory of Collective Bargaining*. P. S. King & Son, Ltd., London, 1930.

Hutt, W. H., "Trade Unions and the Price System." Mimeographed study, Seelisberg, 1949.

Iribarren, Jesus y Jose Luis Gutierrez Garcia, *Cinco Grandes Mesajes*. (*Five Great Messages*. The names of the encyclicals are in Latin; y means and.) Pacem in Terris, Ecclesiam Suam, Populorum Progressio y Constitucion Gaudium et Spes. Library of Christian Authors, Madrid, 1967.

King, Willford I., *The Keys to Prosperity*. Constitution and Free Enterprise Foundation, New York, 1948.

Knight, F. H., "The Determination of Just Wages," reprinted in Hoover, Glenn (Editor), *Twentieth Century Economic Thought*. Philosophical Library, New York, 1950. "The Determination of Just Wages." Mimeographed copy, Seelisberg, 1949.

Lester, Richard A. and Joseph Shister (Editors), *Insights into Labor Issues*. Macmillan, New York, 1948.

Lindblom, Charles E., *Unions and Capitalism*. Yale University Press, London, 1949.

Lopez, Aparicio, Alfonso, *El Movimiento Obrero en Mexico*. (*The Labor Movement in Mexico*.) Mexico, Jus, (Editors), 1952.

Mayo, Elton, *The Social Problems of an Industrial Civilization*. Routledge and Kegan Paul, Ltd., London, 1949.

McNaughton, Wayne L. and Joseph Lazar, *Industrial Relations and the Government*. McGraw-Hill Book Company, New York, 1954.

Messner, Johannes, *La Cuestión Social*. (*The Social Question*.) Rialp Editions, S. A. Madrid, 1960.

Mises, Ludwig von, *Human Action*. Yale University Press, New York, 1949. Henry Regnery Company, Chicago, 1966.

Moulton, Harold G., *Controlling Factors in Economic Development*. The Brookings Institution, Washington, 1949.

National Association of Manufacturers, *The American Individual Enterprise System*. McGraw-Hill Book Company, Inc., New York, 1946.

Petro, Sylvester, *The Labor Policy of the Free Society*. The Ronald Press Company, New York, 1957.

Petro, Sylvester, *Personal Freedom and Labor Policy*. Institute of Economic Affairs, New York University, New York, 1958.

Philbrook, Clarence E. and Salomon Barkin, "Two Views on Why Wages Rise." *The Southern Economic Journal*, October 2, 1957.

Rivera Marin, Guadalupe, *El Mercado de Trabajo*. (*The Labor Market*.) Fondo de Cultura Económica, Mexico, 1955.

Robbins, Lionel, *The Economic Basis of Class Conflict*. Macmillan, London, 1933.

Roberts, B. C., *Trade Unions in a Free Society*. Institute of Economic Affairs, London, 1959.

Robertson, D. J., *A Market for Labour*. The Institute of Economic Affairs, London, 1961.

Robinson, Joan, *Introduction to the Theory of Employment*. Macmillan, London, 1952.

Roel, Carlos, *Estado de Derecho o Huelga*. (*Rule of Law or Strikes*.) Stylo, Mexico, 1942.

Rogers, Thorold, *Six Centuries of Work and Wages*. George Allen and Unwin, Ltd., London, 1949.

Rothschild, K. W., *The Theory of Wages*. Basil Blackwell, Oxford, 1954.

Salceda, Alberto G., *No Puede Existir una Doctrina Social Cristiana*. (*There Can Be No Christian Social Doctrine*.) The Freedom Club, Mexico.

Seldon, Arthur, *Pensions in a Free Society*. Institute of Economic Affairs, London, 1957.

Schultz, George P., *Strikes: The Private Stake and the Public Interest*. University of Chicago Press, Chicago, 1948.

Simons, Henry C., *Economic Policy for a Free Society*. University of Chicago Press, Chicago, 1948.

Slichter, Sumner H., *The Challenge of Industrial Relations*. Cornell University Press, Ithaca, 1947.

Tannenbaum, Frank, *A Philosophy of Labor*. Alfred A. Knopf, New York, 1951.

Watts, Orval V., *Union Monopoly, Its Cause and Cure*. Foundation for Social Research, Los Angeles, 1954.

Williams, Gertrude (Lady), "The Myth of Fair Wages." *Economic Journal*, LXVI, No. 264, 1956.

Wolman, Leo, *Industry-Wide Bargaining*. The Foundation for Economic Education, Irvington-on-Hudson, New York, 1948.

Wright, David McCord, (Editor), *The Impact of the Labor Union*. Harcourt, Brace and Company, New York, 1951.

Zamora, Francisco, *La Lucha contra el Salario*. (*The Struggle against Wages*. Artes Graficas, Mexico, 1949.

Biographical Note

Gustavo R. Velasco was born in Mexico City on April 3, 1903. He attended grammar school in Mexico City and Guadalajara, and high school in Mexico City and Los Angeles, California. From 1922 to 1926 he studied law at the Independent Law School (Escuela Libre de Derecho) in Mexico. In 1925 and 1926 he worked as law clerk in the General Accounting Office of the Mexican Federal Government. From 1927 to 1931 he was second in charge at the Bureau of the Public Domain at the Treasury Department. From mid-1931 to early 1932 he was Chief of the Bureau of the Budget. Since 1932 he has practiced law in a private capacity. Among his clients have been several banks, such as Banco Internacional, S. A., and some 40 deposit banks affiliated with Banco Internacional, department stores, and other important enterprises that do business in Mexico.

Velasco is Vice Chairman of the Board of Directors of Banco Internacional Inmobiliario, S. A., member of the Board of Banco Internacional de Fomento Urbano, S. A. He was Secretary at Banco Internacional, S. A., and Aseguradora Mexicana, S.A., for over 30 years.

Since 1932 Velasco has been Professor of Administrative Law at the Escuela Libre de Derecho and has taught the second year course since 1936. He was a member of the Governing Board from 1937 to 1946 and in 1944 acted as Dean. In 1955 he was again elected Dean by the General Meeting of Professors and occupied this post until 1965 when he resigned.

In 1947–1948 Velasco was President of the Mexican Bar Association. In 1950–1951 he served as President of the Mexican Bankers Association and has been a member of the Executive Committee or of the Board of Directors much of the time since then. He is a full member of the Mexican Academy of Law and

Jurisprudence and of some other scientific and cultural associations. He is also a member of the Honor Councils of the Mexican Bar Association and the Ilustre y Nacional Colegio de Abogados, the oldest association of lawyers in Mexico, founded in 1760.

Since 1961 Velasco has served as a member of the Board of Trustees of the University of the Americas, formerly Mexico City College, and since 1966 has been a Director of the Mexican-American Intercultural Institute.

He has published several legal studies, chiefly on constitutional and administrative law, such as "Administrative Law and the Science of Administration", Evolution of Mexican Administrative Law", "The Commerce Powers of the Federal Government", "Martial Law and Administrative Law", (translated into English and published by the Tulane Law Review), "A Study of the Principles of the Anglo-Saxon Trust", "The Rule of Law in Mexico", included in "Mexico, a Symposium on Law and Government" (published by the University of Miami in 1958).

He has also translated into Spanish books and articles in English, French and Italian, among them "The Federalist" by Hamilton, Madison, and Jay.

Since 1937 Velasco has been interested in the study of economics and has published several articles and lectures, most of which appeared in 1958 under the title of "Libertad y Abundancia" (Freedom and Plenty). He has also been a frequent translator of articles on economics by Mises, Hayek, Röpke, Rueff, and Hazlitt. In September, 1962, he was elected one of the vice-presidents of the Mont Pelerin Society, and in 1965 he was re-elected for a further period of two years.

In 1965 Velasco published "Bibliografia de la Libertad", a list of books and pamphlets in Spanish, favorable to freedom, and a translation into Spanish of "The Economics of Underdeveloped Countries", by P. T. Bauer and B. S. Yamey.

Velasco is a member of the Board of Directors of the Institute for Humane Studies, in Menlo Park, California.

In 1964 Velasco was elected Honorary Dean of the Escuela Libre de Derecho and Honorary President for life of the Mexican Bar Association.